Walks For All Ages North York Moors

WALKS FOR ALL AGES

NORTH YORK MOORS

PAUL HANNON

BRADWELL
BOOKS

Published by Bradwell Books
9 Orgreave Close Sheffield S13 9NP
Email: books@bradwellbooks.co.uk

British Library Cataloguing in Publication Data: a catalogue record for this book is available from the British Library.
1st Edition
ISBN: 9781910551844
Design by: Andy Caffrey
Typesetting and mapping: Mark Titterton
Photograph credits: The author
Front cover image: iStock
Print: Gomer Press, Llandysul, Ceredigion SA44 4JL

The information in this book has been produced in good faith and is intended as a general guide. Although the maps in this book are based on original Ordnance Survey mapping, walkers are always advised to use a detailed OS map. Look in 'The Basics' section for recommendations for the most suitable map for each of the walks
Bradwell Books and the authors have made all reasonable efforts to ensure that the details are correct at the time of publication. Bradwell Books and the authors cannot accept responsibility for any changes that have taken place subsequent to the book being published.
It is the responsibility of individuals undertaking any of the walks listed in this book to exercise due care and consideration for their own health and wellbeing and that of others in their party. The walks in this book are not especially strenuous, but individuals taking part should ensure they are fit and well before setting off.
A good pair of walking books is essential for these walks. It is advisable to take good-quality waterproofs, and if undertaking the walks during the winter, take plenty of warm clothing as well. Because the walks will take some time, it would be a good idea to take along some food and drink.
Enjoy walking. Enjoy the North York Moors with Bradwell Books!

CONTENTS

INTRODUCTION

THE NORTH YORK MOORS NATIONAL PARK COVERS AN AREA OF 553 SQUARE MILES, AND IS THE BEST DEFINED OF ALL THE UPLAND AREAS, RISING ISLAND-LIKE FROM THE SURROUNDING COUNTRYSIDE. THIS CREATES AN IMPRESSION OF MUCH GREATER ALTITUDE THAN ITS MODEST HIGH POINT OF 1489FT/454M ATTAINS.

To the north is the Cleveland Plain, westwards the Vales of Mowbray and York, and southwards the Vale of Pickering, while to the east is the ultimate low point, the North Sea.

The park itself however has a solid upland mass spreading from the centre towards the western escarpments, where one can walk for mile upon mile and lose little altitude. It is of course all this heather-clad moorland for which the National Park is best known.

Heather moors, despite their profusion, are only one aspect of this diverse region, for here are lush green valleys and a spectacular length of coastline composed largely of rugged cliffs. There are sandy beaches and rocky coves, and inland some shapely summits, fascinating rock outcrops and beautiful waterfalls, while enchanting indigenous woods remain in addition to large forests. The hand of man has been everywhere, for even the lonely moortops are littered with ancient burial mounds and standing stones. The scores of delightful villages range from fishing ports to moorland farming communities, though many villages take advantage of the shelter beneath the hills.

Man has also left ruined abbeys and castles; some old roads including drovers' routes, a Roman road and numerous paved trods; absorbing relics of the former ironstone, alum and jet industries; and not least of all an unrivalled collection of wayside crosses, some being ancient Christian symbols, others serving as waymarks or boundary stones. This is walkers' territory par excellence, with a plethora of long distance and challenge walks crossing it. Best known are the Cleveland Way and the Lyke Wake Walk, while the Coast to Coast Walk ends its classic journey here.

To the north of the central dome, the park's major river, the Esk, flows east to the coast at Whitby, and absorbs many short tributaries including Westerdale, Danby Dale, the Fryup Dales, Glaisdale and the valleys of the Murk Esk and Little Beck. The main valley has characterful villages strung along its entire length, including Danby, Lealholm and Egton Bridge. Flowing south from the dome, a string of parallel valleys divided by high moorland ridges include Ryedale, Bilsdale, Bransdale, Farndale and Rosedale, all squeezing between the unassuming Tabular Hills. The undulating whaleback ridge of the Hambleton Hills delineates the western boundary above the Vale of Mowbray, fusing into the Cleveland Hills, which rise more aggressively above the Cleveland Plain. Scattered liberally around the area is a lovely range of villages such as Rievaulx, Hutton-le-Hole and Rosedale Abbey. To the east meanwhile, the cliffs rise dramatically and support old fishing communities such as Robin Hood's Bay and Staithes tumbling to the shore.

The area is bordered by Scarborough to the south-east, Northallerton to the west and Middlesbrough to the north, while more closely involved are the market towns of Thirsk, Helmsley, Kirkbymoorside, Pickering, Stokesley and Guisborough.

NORTH YORK MOORS NATIONAL PARK
PUBLIC PATH TO
HIGH MILL
POST OFFICE
WED

1 RIEVAULX

RIEVAULX ABBEY DATES FROM THE 12TH CENTURY AND VIES WITH THAT OTHER GREAT YORKSHIRE HOUSE OF THE CISTERCIANS, FOUNTAINS ABBEY, IN THE BEAUTY OF ITS WOODED ENVIRONS. THERE IS HOWEVER A VERY IMPOSING GRANDEUR HERE THAT IS PERHAPS UNPARALLELED: A LEISURELY, REFLECTIVE AMBLE AROUND ITS REMAINS IS GUARANTEED TO RESTORE INNER PEACE.

Perhaps not surprisingly the abbey took over a century to build, yet it is still difficult to imagine how something so majestic could have been created with the rudimentary tools available at that time. It is now in the care of English Heritage. High on the hillside above (reached by continuing up the lane through the hamlet - note the thatched cottages) are the delightfully laid out Rievaulx Terraces, complete with two temples. Created by the Duncombe family in the 18th century, the National Trust now maintains that site.

The name Rievaulx is derived from its Norman founders, referring to 'Rye' and 'Valley'. The River Rye is the second most important river of the North York Moors, running some 38 miles from its beginnings amid the high moors above Hawnby. Flowing down through Rievaulx and Helmsley, it then absorbs a string of neighbouring rivers in the Vale of Pickering before being absorbed by the River Derwent just short of Malton.

THE BASICS

Distance: 3½ miles / 5.5km

Gradient: One short climb through Ashberry Wood

Severity: Easy walking

Approx. time to walk: 2 to 2½ hours

Stiles: None

Maps: OS Landranger 100 (Malton & Pickering); Explorer OL26 (North York Moors Western area)

Path description: Fieldpaths and quiet lanes and tracks

Start Point: Rievaulx village centre (GR SE 575849)

Parking: Car park (refund for abbey visitors), roadside parking (PC YO62 5LB)

Dog friendly: Sheep pastures, dogs preferably on leads

Public toilets: At start

Nearest food: Tearoom at start

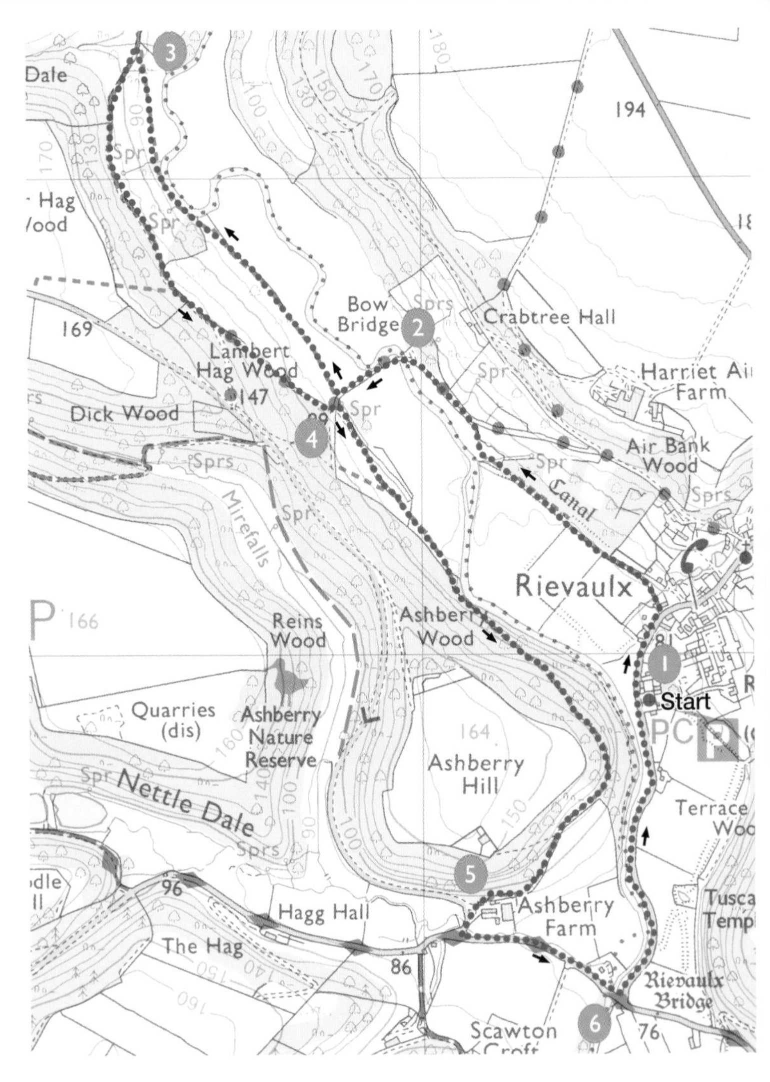

THE ROUTE

1. From the abbey take the road north into the hamlet, and after a handful of buildings take a gate on the left ('footpath to Bow Bridge'). Cross a stable yard and a paddock before continuing away alongside a hedge. Just over it are the scant remains of a canal that brought quarried stone to the abbey construction site. A grassy path heads away with a hedge on the right, then along a fenceside. This straight line leads to the bank of the River Rye. A sketchy path heads upstream, but with Bow Bridge visible ahead, leave the river for a bridle-gate onto an enclosed track which drops down to the shapely bridge.

2. Shortly after crossing it, before the track starts to scale the wooded bank, take a gate on the right and a path heads away alongside a fence beneath a scrubby bank. At the end the river is rejoined, and traced on boardwalks through a steep wooded bank. Emerging, forsake the river again as the path crosses straight over the pasture to a gate onto the farm road to Tylas.

3. Double back left on this, rising away to run beneath steep, colourful slopes of scattered scrub. It runs on to a fork at Lambert Hag Wood: this is a good point to look back over the valley. While the access road begins a steep climb to the through road, escape instead along the left branch, a rough road that slants down beneath wooded slopes. As it swings left at the bottom you are just a few paces short of the outward route near Bow Bridge.

4. Before it, however, take a gate on the right and head away on a level path beneath a grassy bank. Through a gate/stile it continues beneath a wooded bank to approach a bend of the River Rye. Just before it, take a gate in front from where the broad path slants up through Ashberry Wood. In stages of differing gradients it reaches a brow where another way comes in from the right. There are intermittent glimpses through the trees of Rievaulx Abbey during this stage. At once a gentle slant back down begins, but the path quickly levels out and curves round to the right, latterly with open fields below giving nice views over Ryedale. At a fork take the left option, recommencing a nice slant down the wood bottom to emerge into the yard at Ashberry Farm, and out to join a road.

5. Go left over the bridge, then left again (note the old North Riding roadsign). The farm makes a lovely picture, as does the scene by the cottage at Rievaulx Bridge, five minutes further.

6. Across the bridge turn left along the road back to the beckoning abbey. Part way on, a short section of path offers an unofficial stroll with the Rye.

2 SUTTON BANK

SUTTON BANK IS A WELL-KNOWN NAME IN NORTH YORKSHIRE, WHERE THE HAIRPIN BENDS OF THE A170 CLIMB FROM THE PLAINS TO THE HAMBLETON ESCARPMENT: THIS IS THE ONLY MAIN ROAD TO TACKLE THE HAMBLETON HILLS, THOUGH ITS ONCE FEARFUL REPUTATION IS NOW CHIEFLY HISTORICAL. GIVEN A COMPETENT DRIVER MODERN CARS HAVE LITTLE DIFFICULTY, THOUGH LARGER VEHICLES STILL OCCASIONALLY COME UNSTUCK. IN DENSE WOODLAND AT THE FOOT OF THE HILLS LIES GORMIRE LAKE IN A DEEP HOLLOW: WITH NEITHER FEEDER NOR OUTLET, AT ONE TIME IT WAS THOUGHT TO BE BOTTOMLESS!

Whitestone Cliff's substantial limestone crags provide an early classic moment, with the waters of Gormire Lake sat below amid a dramatic couch of greenery. Beyond it are the red-roofed villages of Felixkirk and further north, Boltby beneath the backdrop of its forest. Looking back south beyond Sutton Bank is the vertical plunge of Roulston Scar. Hambleton Down, on your right, once boasted a racecourse, and this remains a major racehorse training area.

The White Horse of Kilburn is a landmark of great Yorkshire pride. This amazing creature was the brainchild of businessman Thomas Taylor: over 300 feet long, it was carved out of the hillside by the village schoolmaster in 1857. What sets this apart from its southern cousins is the fact that its base is not of chalk, and consequently requires regular upkeep. Its very size means it is more satisfactorily appraised from the vicinity of the village than when you're actually up here! The views out, however, are far-reaching, looking south over the Howardian Hills to the more distant line of the Yorkshire Wolds.

At the foot of the White Horse, Kilburn village is home to another famous Yorkshire 'pet', for at its hub are the workshops begun by Robert Thompson, the 'Mouseman', where the little carved mouse climbs his furniture. This delightful trademark can be found in numerous churches, pubs and houses in and beyond the county.

The Yorkshire Gliding Club is another well-known feature of the Sutton Bank area, and regularly provides a colourful and animated scene. The graceful movements of gliders are often in evidence in the skies above, more impressive still if one should be towed into the air straight over your head when stood on Roulston Scar. Like Whitestone Cliff before it, the scar gives magnificent views westward across the Vale of Mowbray to the Yorkshire Dales.

If you decide against dropping down to the lake, this is a linear walk, taking in the dramatic setting of Gormire Lake and the quirky White Horse at opposite ends of the walk.

THE BASICS

Distance: 4¾ miles / 7.5km (4¼ miles / 6.75km if omitting lake)

Gradient: Level walking if omitting lake section, otherwise a sustained steep descent and re-ascent

Severity: Very easy if omitting lake section, otherwise a demanding uphill section (though on a good path)

Approx. time to walk: 3 hours (2½ if omitting lake section)

Stiles: None

Maps: OS Landranger 100 (Malton & Pickering); Explorer OL26 (North York Moors Western area)

Path description: Firm escarpment and steep woodland paths

Start Point: Sutton Bank National Park Centre (GR SE 515830)

Parking: National Park car park (PC YO7 2EH)

Dog friendly: Yes

Public toilets: At start

Nearest food: Tearoom at start

2 SUTTON BANK WALK

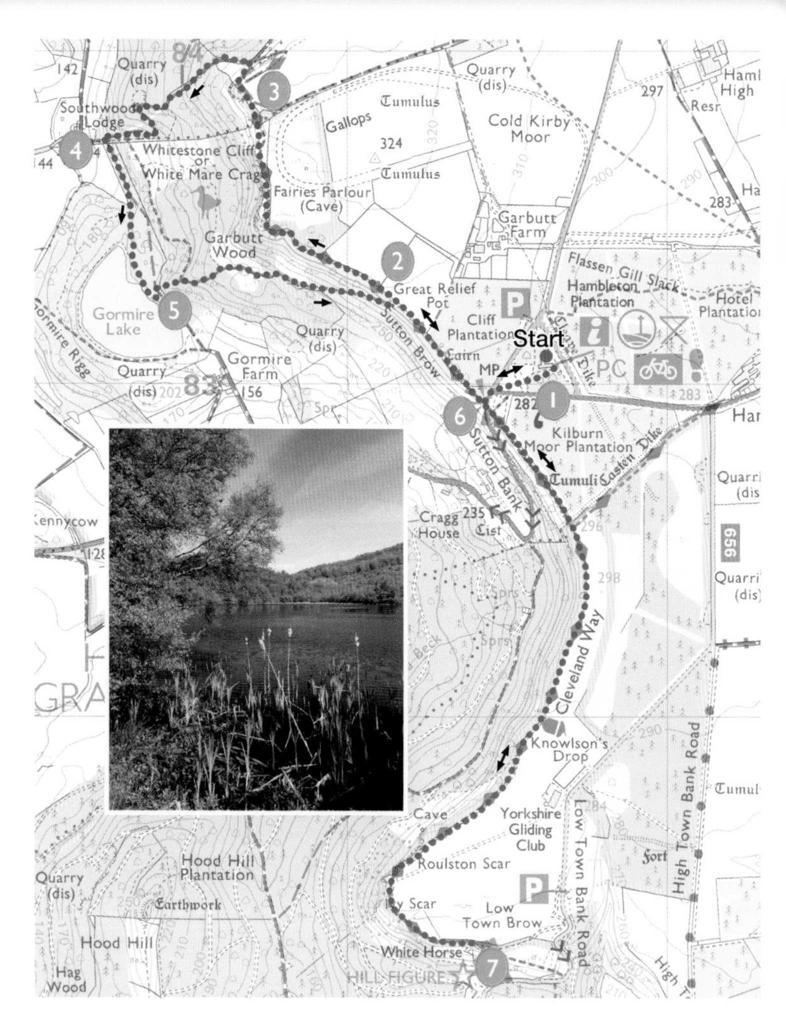

THE ROUTE

1. Cross the car park on the Sutton Bank side of the visitor centre, joining a firm path that crosses the Cold Kirby road just where it leaves the main road at the rim of Sutton Bank. A very popular, firm path runs to the right, along the near-level escarpment to a platform proclaiming the 'Finest view in England'. Gormire Lake is seen in its entirety far below. You are joined by a parallel bridleway. A minute further, ignore a path departing steeply left: this is your return route – should you wish to accept it!

2. A dead-flat stride now opens out with fantastic views. Through a short section of woodland the path emerges onto Whitestone Cliff, with a seat on the open plinth to your left – take care with young children. Just further, a more airy plinth looks

north along the scar. Beyond Whitestone Cliff you drop slightly to a promontory with another seat to look back along the scar and over the lake. The separate bridleway ends here, and unless you are undertaking the far more demanding full walk visiting Gormire Lake, then this is the point to return from. Retrace your steps to Sutton Bank and pick up the instructions at waypoint 6.

3. If opting for the full walk, then advance on the firm edge path past a three-way bridleway sign, and within five minutes another bridleway junction is reached. Here take the grassy one doubling back left into the wooded Thirlby Bank. Quickly dropping to a shelf beneath crags, it briefly runs on before commencing a big descent. Through an old wall it slants left down through the wood, partly on the rim of a deep hollowed way. The path swings sharply back right and down to another waymarked bridleway junction at the foot.

4. Just a few strides below is Southwoods Lodge, but your way remains in the trees, on a broad path doubling back left and rising very slightly before undulating through the woods to quickly approach Gormire Lake. With the lakeshore on your right, you quickly reach a signed path junction.

5. Take the one climbing steeply left, and quickly entering Garbutt Wood, branch right at a signed path junction to rise less severely. It levels out and runs by a massive, square boulder, then recommences its uphill slant, opening out from the trees to restore big views and ultimately rejoin the outward path on the escarpment. The top of Sutton Bank is now only five minutes along to the right.

6. On regaining the road at Sutton Bank top you could opt to finish, but would miss the **easiest two-mile return walk along** the level rim to visit the White Horse. Cross straight over the road at the bank top onto another firm path to walk the few strides to a topograph surveying the panorama. For the White Horse, simply trace the dead-level path for virtually a mile around the rim of the escarpment, with a gliding club appearing to your left. With Roulston Scar then Ivy Scar down to your right, the path ultimately swings left to arrive at the top of the White Horse.

7. To finish simply retrace your steps back to Sutton Bank.

3 OSMOTHERLEY

OSMOTHERLEY HAS A HIGHLY ATTRACTIVE VILLAGE CENTRE WHERE A SMALL GREEN MARKS A MEETING OF ROADS LINED BY STONE COTTAGES, THE MAIN STREET SLOPING THROUGHOUT ITS LENGTH. ON THE GREEN IS A MARKET CROSS, NEXT TO WHICH IS A STONE TABLE WHERE JOHN WESLEY PREACHED: JUST AROUND THE BACK IS HIS EARLY METHODIST CHAPEL OF 1754.

Almost everything has a central position, with the church of St Peter showing traces of Norman work, and three pubs. There are also tearooms, shop, fish-shop, youth hostel and an annual agricultural show. As a starting point for the infamous Lyke Wake Walk, Osmotherley has an indefinable ramblers' atmosphere.

The Lyke Wake Walk is a gruelling 42-mile march across the entire breadth of the North York Moors, concluding at Ravenscar on the distant coast. Devised by a legendary figure of the Moors, the late Bill Cowley, its origins are steeped in the tradition of long-distance coffin-bearing routes. Though its popularity has waned since its heyday of the 1970s, it remains a hugely challenging expedition to be completed within 24 hours. Its onward route is encountered briefly in these pages on the Carlton Bank and Clay Bank Top walks.

Chequers Farm at Slape Stones was once an inn serving cattle drovers: note the sign affixed to the outside wall. Though refreshments and a farm shop replaced it, today all is quiet.

Rising beyond here is the moorland prow of Black Hambleton, very much the dominant feature of this walk. At 1312ft/400m this is the highest point of the Hambleton Hills, which form a very distinct western boundary to the National Park, overlooking the flat plains of the Vale of Mowbray. Oak Dale takes a deep bite into the shoulder of Black Hambleton. Its upper reservoir was drained in 2014 and the area is returning to a more natural appearance. Beyond Oak Dale Farm you have a glimpse of the surviving Oakdale Lower Reservoir.

THE BASICS

Distance: 5 miles / 8km

Gradient: One appreciable uphill section near start

Severity: Generally easy walking

Approx. time to walk: 3 hours

Stiles: Three

Maps: OS Landranger 99 (Northallerton & Ripon), Landranger 100 (Malton & Pickering); Explorer OL26 (North York Moors Western area)

Path description: Moorland and field paths

Start Point: Osmotherley village centre (GR SE 456972)

Parking: Roadside parking (PC DL6 3AA)

Dog friendly: Sheep pastures and moorland, dogs preferably on leads, make sure they can manage the stiles

Public toilets: At start

Nearest food: Pubs at start

3 OSMOTHERLEY WALK

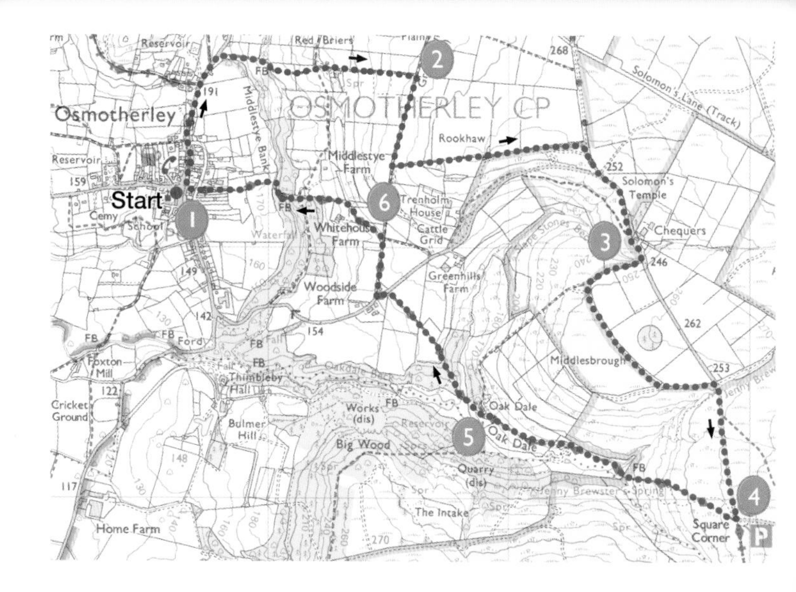

THE ROUTE

1. Leave the village centre by the Swainby road rising due north. On easing out advance just past the de-restriction sign then turn right down a rough, enclosed track. This drops to a ford and bridge on Cod Beck, then climbs steeply away. As it forks keep straight up to the farm above. Through gates to its left escape into a field above, then ascend the hedgeside to a gate onto aptly named Green Lane.

2. Turn right through a gate/stile to enjoy a colourful, enclosed level stroll. Just as the lane starts to drop gently away take a stile on the left, cross a horse track to a small gate and a path climbs away alongside an old wall. Through a gate/stile at the top the going eases. Advance along the fieldside with the wall, but just short of the corner gate, take a stile in a gateway on your right into open country. Black Hambleton rises beyond the deep bowl of Slape Stones Beck. A little path goes left to meet a grassy cart track, which runs alongside a fence onto a road. Turn right onto the Osmotherley-Hawnby road, then left as far as the house at Chequers.

3. Immediately beyond Chequers take a wallside track to the right back onto moorland. When the wall turns off left after a gate/stile, go with it on a lesser track, which beyond a few reeds joins a better grassy track rising from the main one. Go left

on this, rising slightly and tracing that wall all the way, over a heathery brow and gently down to a gate. Through this a firmer track is joined and followed left, still with the wall back onto the road. Turn right, and with a useful verge this crosses the moor to a car park at a sharp bend at Oakdale Head under Black Hambleton.

4. Here you join the Cleveland Way which will lead all the way back. This takes the firm path dropping right across the moor, through bracken and heather. Soon becoming stone surfaced, it descends into the trees of Oak Dale. Over a small footbridge an access road is joined, leading out past a former reservoir and down to Oak Dale Farm.

5. Resume down this rough road, crossing a bridge at a sheltered corner then climbing steeply to run along to a road at a lone house. Drop briefly left then take a farm drive climbing right. It quickly eases and runs on to swing left down towards White House Farm. Just before it your path contours across a steep field bottom on the right, passing above the farm.

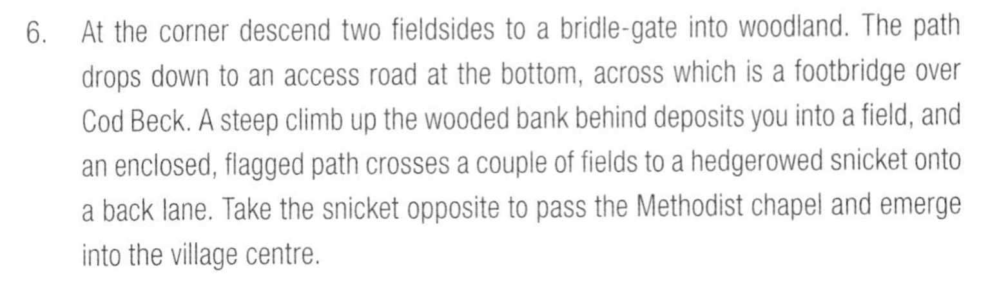

6. At the corner descend two fieldsides to a bridle-gate into woodland. The path drops down to an access road at the bottom, across which is a footbridge over Cod Beck. A steep climb up the wooded bank behind deposits you into a field, and an enclosed, flagged path crosses a couple of fields to a hedgerowed snicket onto a back lane. Take the snicket opposite to pass the Methodist chapel and emerge into the village centre.

4 CARLTON BANK

HIGH ABOVE THE LOVELY VILLAGE OF CARLTON-IN-CLEVELAND, THE SUMMIT OF CARLTON BANK BOASTS AN INTELLIGENTLY HIDDEN CAFÉ AND CAR PARK. THE FORMER IS A PARTICULAR BOON TO LONG DISTANCE WALKERS AS IT OFFERS THE ONLY ON-ROUTE REFRESHMENT TO CLEVELAND WAYFARERS BETWEEN OSMOTHERLEY AND KILDALE; AND TO COAST TO COASTERS BETWEEN INGLEBY ARNCLIFFE AND THE LION INN AT BLAKEY. LORD STONES IS NAMED FROM A BRONZE AGE BURIAL MOUND NOW VERY OVERGROWN NEAR THE ROAD.

Cringle End is one of those indefinable 'good places to be'. Perched on its airy promontory are a memorial topograph and seat and also an old boundary stone. Here a mild surprise awaits, for the ground continues rising further still, in dramatic fashion past the summit of Cringle Moor. Looking back Carlton Moor presents a fine shape, due in part to the old quarries on its steep north face.

At 1417ft/432m, Cringle Moor is the second highest point on the North York Moors, and is a good deal shapelier than the superior Round Hill on Urra Moor - though in step with its loftier cousin its summit mound remains largely undisturbed by the passing multitudes. The path above the dramatic plunge of its steep northern face boasts an uninterrupted view of the Cleveland Plain and the fellow Cleveland Hills.

Spoil heaps encountered on the walk are from former jet mines, this once being a much favoured ornamental stone. It was at its most popular in the 19th century, and worn with zeal by Queen Victoria during the extended mourning over her beloved Prince Albert. Along with jet – which was more commonly mined on the coast around Whitby - these hills were also plundered for alum and ironstone. Evidence of the old workings abounds; good examples hereabouts being neatly arrayed along the same contour. The splendid return path is along a route used by 19th century jet miners.

THE BASICS

Distance: 3 miles / 4.75km

Gradient: One short, stone surfaced climb onto Cringle End

Severity: Easy walking

Approx. time to walk: 2 to 2½ hours

Stiles: None

Maps: OS Landranger 93 (Middlesbrough & Darlington); Explorer OL26 (North York Moors Western area)

Path description: Good moorland footpaths

Start Point: Carlton Bank (GR NZ 523030)

Parking: Car park at Lord Stones Country Park on summit of Carlton-Chop Gate road (PC TS9 7JH)

Dog friendly: Moorland, dogs preferably on leads

Public toilets: WCs at cafe

Nearest food: Café at start

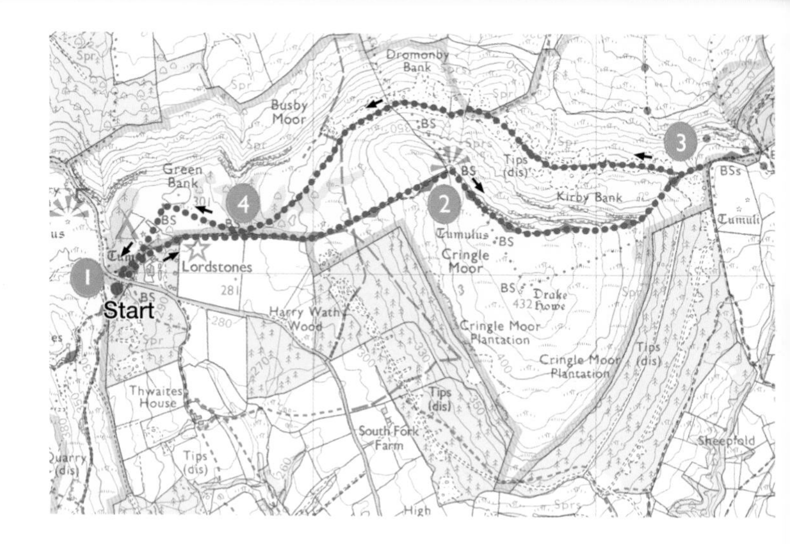

THE ROUTE

1. Leave the car park by the rear, emerging alongside WCs onto the Cleveland Way path. This runs along to the right to follow a fence along the edge of this open area with scattered clumps of alien conifers. Approaching denser trees the way forks: the left branch will be your return route. For now keep right on an enclosed path to a bridle-gate. Here a stone-built path climbs in the company of a wall to gain the prominent furniture on Cringle End, a place to linger.

2. The flagged path enjoys a fine walk along the northern scarp, though all too soon the steep descent begins. Also rebuilt, this is a vast improvement on a once badly eroded and dangerous section. Passing through a few spoil heaps near the bottom, a junction with a path coming in from the left is reached just two minutes short of a wall corner at Kirby Bank. This is your return route, but first, advance to the wall corner. Just 75 strides further, and immediately before a fork, is a stubby old guidepost in a base inscribed 'Kirby Road North'.

3. Returning to the wall corner and the path junction, now bear right on the 'natural' path. After surmounting an old spoil heap your path sets off on an excellent stroll

around the northern, bracken-draped slopes of Cringle Moor, far below your outward route. The objective at the far end under Cringle End is clear, the path gently dipping and then rising slightly before attaining that point. A fence comes up to run parallel just below, bringing briefly green pasture beneath it. Further, your path passes through a bridle-gate/stile in the now ascending fence and continues on to a signed path junction where the side options are barely discernible. Just a minute further, an unsigned major cross-paths junction is reached. Again simply keep straight on your main path, dropping gently down to enter conifers and quickly rejoining the outward path at the foot of its ascent.

4. Although you can simply retrace your steps back to the start, or opt for a modest variation finish. This quickly forks right into more open grassland, with an option to bear further right up to a modern semi-circle of 5 stones on the brow – one features an intriguing carving. After a last view over the Cleveland Plain, a grassy path slants back down to the start.

CROSS FELL
PENSHAW
WEARDALE
TEESDALE
STAINMOOR
DARLINGTON
SHUNNER FELL
SWALEDALE
RICHMOND
WHERNSIDE
INGLEBOROUGH
PENHILL
WHORLHILL
BY HIS
IN
1884 - ALEC

HARTLEPOOL
SEAL SANDS
TEES-MOUTH
WILTON
UPLEATHAM
BARNABY MOOR
ROSEBERRY TOPPING
EASBY HILL
KILDALE
PARK NAB
TURKEY NAB
EAT
ED
RIENDS
OF
CONER - 1968

5 CLAY BANK TOP

CLAY BANK IS THE STEEP CLIMB TAKEN BY THE BUSY B1257 FROM THE CLEVELAND PLAIN, THROUGH THE PASS OF CLAY BANK TOP AND DOWN INTO BILSDALE. THE MAGNIFICENTLY SITED CAR PARK, VIRTUALLY AT THE TOP, ALLOWS MOTORISTS TO SURVEY THE PLAIN AND THE UNMISTAKABLE PEAK OF ROSEBERRY TOPPING FROM THEIR CAR WINDOWS. REFRESHMENTS ARE OFTEN AVAILABLE HERE.

The western section of the Cleveland Hills, namely Carlton Moor, Cringle Moor, Cold Moor and Hasty Bank form an irresistible switchback of shapely hills, and are a joy to tread. From Garfit Gap back to Clay Bank Top you trace the route of the long-established Cleveland Way National Trail, along with the country's most famous, though unofficial trail, the Coast to Coast Walk. The popularity of these walks has seen most of its journey over the particularly appealing Cleveland Hills being given a solid stone surface to prevent further erosion.

Though not the highest point on the Cleveland ridge, Hasty Bank is arguably the finest. The splendid path clings to its northern rim, where some appreciably craggy edges fall steeply north: here the flat Cleveland Plain contrasts sharply with Bilsdale stretching away to the south. The Wain Stones are Hasty Bank's pride and joy, a tumbled group of crags and boulders popular with rock climbers and one of the most impressive features of the North York Moors.

Bilsdale is one of the longest valleys of the National Park, commencing in the lap of the Cleveland Hills and running south between high moorland walls. Its lower slopes however present a charming pastoral scene in which a surprising number of farms appear to survive as if in a time warp. Bilsdale's river, the unassuming Seph, is absorbed by the Rye near Hawnby, which then flows out of the moors towards Rievaulx and Helmsley.

THE BASICS

Distance: 2¾ miles / 4.5km

Gradient: Undulating with one easy uphill section

Severity: Moderate

Approx. time to walk: 2 to 2½ hours

Stiles: Three

Maps: OS Landranger 93 (Middlesbrough & Darlington); Explorer OL26 (North York Moors Western area)

Path description: Rough pasture and solid moorland paths

Start Point: Clay Bank Top on B1257 Helmsley-Stokesley road. (GR NZ 571035)

Parking: Forestry Commission car park (PC TS9 7JA)

Dog friendly: Sheep pastures and moorland, dogs preferably on leads, make sure they can manage the stiles

Public toilets: None

Nearest food: Pubs at Chop Gate and Great Broughton

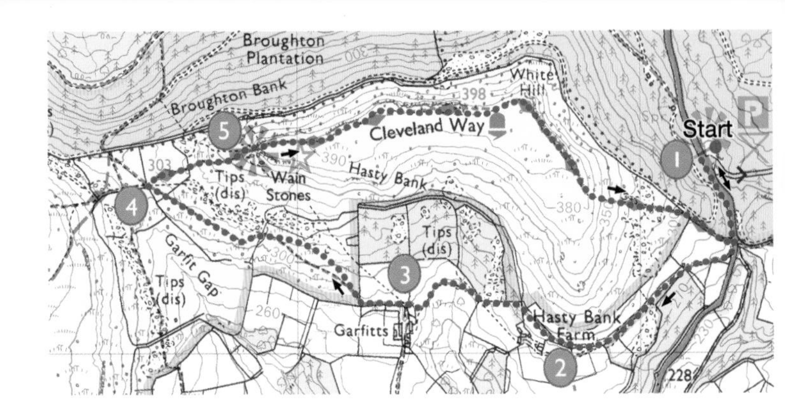

THE ROUTE

1. From the car park head briefly south along the road to its brow, and with caution cross to where the Cleveland Way's stepped route ascends steeply right. This is to be your return route, so for now advance just two paces further and take the Hasty Bank Farm road on the right. Through a gate/stile follow it rising away to another gate/stile, then leveling out to curve through scattered woodland with increasingly good views down Bilsdale.

2. Soon reaching the farm gate, instead bear right on an inviting grassy path above the wall. This runs on above the house and grounds, beneath colourful slopes and on a little further to a corner. Here take a stile on the left into rough pasture and descend a wallside, a thin path dropping through bracken outside a plantation to a bottom corner stile. Through this the thin path bears away right, through a part wooded, part felled slope, quickly crossing moist terrain on boardwalks. Across, the path bears left, curving around a bracken slope and along towards the farm at Garfitts just ahead.

3. Just short of the grounds, the path turns sharp right to rise to a bridle-gate. Head directly away alongside a fence on your right. As the wall below drops away, keep on to a gateway/stile in an old wall, entering Open Access land. Just above to your right now the mercurial Wain Stones appear, with the long ridge of Cold Moor directly ahead. With the reedy hollow in front offering an unappealing proposition, rise right just as far as the wood corner, then make use of a grassy quad track slanting up to the left. This rises in the Wain Stones' direction, but soon reaches a contouring fence. It turns left with this, dropping briefly and running to a corner gate/stile in a wall ahead. The track continues away alongside a fence, still rising slightly above old spoil heaps and curving neatly around to the right to a gate/stile in a wall.

4. Just below you is the dip of Garfit Gap, while just a few strides to your right is a bridle-gate where you join the stone-floored course of the Cleveland Way. Pass through and make the very short ascent to the initially unseen rock pinnacles of the Wain Stones. The path picks an easy way between the boulders to gain the western edge of Hasty Bank's lengthy top.

5. Now the stone path heads eastwards to commence the level crossing of the long plateau. Towards the end the adjacent cliffs are of a serious scale, emphasized by an unbroken fall from just off the path. The descent is again steep, beginning at the end of the cliffs and dropping through a few spoil heaps to join a forestry track at a kissing-gate. Instead of following the track, the stone path continues down by the wall to emerge back onto the road at Clay Bank Top. Cross with care to finish.

6 WESTERDALE

SUPERB MOORLAND PATHS LEAD IN AND OUT OF THE HIDDEN VALLEY OF BAYSDALE. IMMENSELY SECLUDED, IT APPEARS VERY HAPPY TO REMAIN LOCKED AWAY FROM THE OUTSIDE WORLD. JUST A LITTLE FURTHER UP-DALE FROM THE WALK IS BAYSDALE ABBEY, A FARM ON THE SITE OF A 12TH CENTURY CISTERCIAN NUNNERY. ROAD ACCESS TO THE DALE IS VIA KILDALE, FURTHER WEST. BAYSDALE BECK DOUBLES THE STRENGTH OF THE EQUALLY YOUTHFUL ESK A MILE AND A HALF FURTHER DOWNSTREAM FROM HOB HOLES, EN ROUTE TO UPPER ESKDALE'S PRINCIPAL VILLAGE OF CASTLETON.

Westerdale is the first village on the River Esk, and gives its name to the valley's uppermost reach in preference to 'Eskdale'. Its buildings cling to the street rising from the river to the moor, and include Christ Church. This peaceful backwater is quieter still since the Victorian pile of Westerdale Hall, once a shooting lodge, closed its doors to youth hostellers in 1992.

Hob Hole is a charming spot in the valley bottom, where the moorland road from Westerdale to Kildale crosses lovely Baysdale Beck by means of a setted - though normally dry – ford. Downstream is a footbridge for when the water level is sufficient to need avoiding. With a large parking area alongside the stream, this is a long-established, popular picnic spot for families. A hob, incidentally, was a goblin-like character peculiar to this region: some were mischievous, others had healing powers.

THE BASICS

Distance: 4¾ miles / 7.5km

Gradient: A steep road start and a gentler uphill mid-walk

Severity: Generally easy walking

Approx. time to walk: 3 hours

Stiles: None

Maps: OS Landranger 94 (Whitby); Explorer OL26 (North York Moors Western area)

Path description: Good paths, largely on moorland

Start Point: Hob Hole (GR NZ 652074)

Parking: Parking area by the beck, on the moorland road from Westerdale towards Kildale 1.5 miles north of Westerdale village) (PC YO21 2DT)

Dog friendly: Moorland and sheep pastures, dogs preferably on leads

Public toilets: In Westerdale village

Nearest food: Pubs and cafes at Castleton, 2½ miles

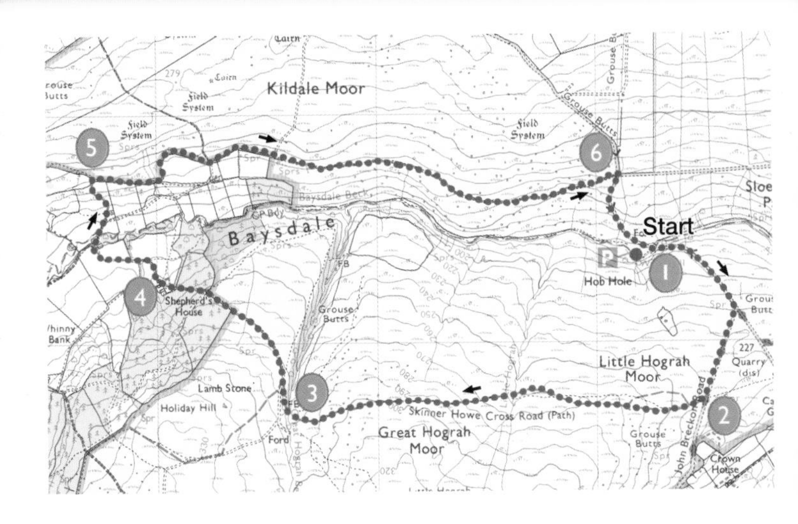

THE ROUTE

1. From the parking area cross Baysdale Beck – by ford or footbridge - to commence a steep but brief pull up the road on the other side. A gentle rise then quickly leads to a fork. Take the lesser branch to the right, known as John Breckon Road. Just beyond the brow, leave by a bridleway on the right.

2. This runs up onto Little Hograh Moor. With intermittent superfluous cairns, this way known as Skinner Howe Cross Road remains your route for some time, rising gently and soon leveling out to reveal most of the walk ahead and across the valley. Dropping to cross Little Hograh, it's gently up again to a brow revealing Great Hograh Beck below and Roseberry Topping far ahead right. From a memorial cairn of 1981 atop a large boulder your path drops to meet the beck at a lovely spot: it is crossed by a delightful little arched bridge with a 1938 inscribed keystone, and a welcome if incongruous seat. The bridge marks the upper limit of the beck's enclosing foliage, emphasized by a sprawling, gnarled oak tree immediately beneath it.

3. Across the bridge, ignore the rougher direct path, and take a nicer, thin one slanting right, quickly rising to deposit you onto a shooters' track. Turn right on this, soon swinging away from the gill and dropping to a gate into a plantation. A quick descent leads to The Low House (Shepherd's House on maps). Avoid its confines by a gate on the right just before a barn, and then curve left around to join its access road.

4. Turn down this as it works its way down to the valley floor. Immediately behind a modern barn, leave by a gate on the right, and a grass track doubles quickly back to a wooden farm bridge on Baysdale Beck. Across, the grassy way slants up towards a low barn, then doubles back uphill to enter bracken at the top. Just set back is a bridle-gate in a wall onto the open country of Kildale Moor.

5. Grass tracks go both ways: yours is the one to the right. The path shadows the wall for a good while, cutting a small corner before reaching another junction outside an old barn, where a branch rises away left. Keep straight on, the wall soon dropping away to a plantation. This leaves your way to run delightfully across the moor, at a lower level than the outward route opposite. The broad path drops a little further before a short rise suddenly deposits you onto a moorland road junction.

6. Turn right down the road to arrive back at Hob Hole in the valley bottom.

7 DANBY

THIS WALK EXPLORES THE HEART OF ESKDALE, THE MAJOR VALLEY OF THE NORTH YORK MOORS NATIONAL PARK. THE RIVER ESK IS THEREFORE THE PRINCIPAL RIVER OF THE PARK, AND FLOWS FOR ALMOST 30 MILES EASTWARDS FROM THE HIGH MOORS, THROUGH LUSH FARMING PASTURES TO EMPTY INTO THE NORTH SEA IN DRAMATIC STYLE AT WHITBY. A STRING OF REGULARLY PLACED VILLAGES, NEVER MORE THAN A COUPLE OF MILES APART, ADD GREATLY TO THE VALLEY'S MANY CHARMS, WHICH INCLUDE A SPLENDIDLY SCENIC RAILWAY LINE TERMINATING, LIKE THE ESK ITSELF, AT WHITBY.

Danby is a scattered settlement whose focal point is Dale End crossroads. Here are the Duke of Wellington pub, a bakery/tearoom and health shop. Danby has one of the last remaining Courts Leet in the country, a relic from manorial days when villagers met to decide local issues. Alongside the Methodist Chapel is the Victoria Jubilee school with a sundial of 1811. Just east of the village is Danby Lodge, originally a shooting lodge of the Dawnays. Today it serves as a major visitor centre for the National Park – the Moors Centre. It stands in a fine setting and lovely grounds, and provides information, displays, shop, café and WCs.

The Pannierman's Causeway is one of countless historic trade routes that thread the valley sides and moortops of Eskdale. Many feature stone slabbed surfaces, important in keeping the route passable for packhorses in unfavourable weather conditions, and a joy for us modern travellers to tread. The walk enjoys glorious views to a succession of ridges and side valleys across Eskdale from some delightful heather moorland, including Danby Rigg, Danby Dale, Castleton Rigg and Castleton village.

THE BASICS

Distance: 3½ miles / 5.5km

Gradient: Modest uphill sections

Severity: Generally easy walking

Approx. time to walk: 2½ hours

Stiles: Three

Maps: OS Landranger 94 (Whitby); Explorer OL26 (North York Moors Western area)

Path description: Largely good moorland paths and tracks

Start Point: Danby village centre (GR NZ 707086)

Parking: Parking area east of pub crossroads (PC YO21 2LY)

Dog friendly: Sheep pastures, dogs preferably on leads, make sure they can manage the stiles

Public toilets: At start

Nearest food: Pub and tearoom at start; café at Danby Lodge nearby

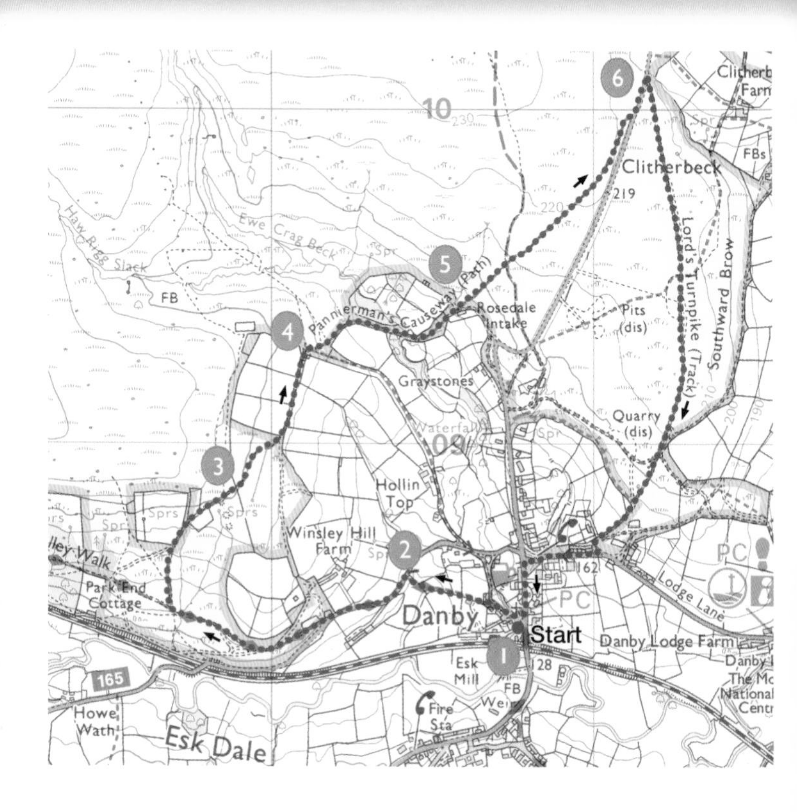

THE ROUTE

1. From the crossroads head down the street towards the station, but turn right past a Methodist chapel at Bridge Green. Across a bridge an access road rises above the stream, shadowed by a stone causeway. Towards the top take a stile on the left, and an enclosed path runs to a gate into a field, remaining enclosed to a small gate at the end. Cross the field bottom to a stile in a section of wall, and from a fence-stile just beyond, cross a sloping field to a stream at a corner gate. Ascend the fieldside to a gate/stile onto a road.

2. Go briefly left, and as it opens out and starts to drop away, take a grassy way right. This crosses an access road then runs as a broad track onto bracken slopes. Ignoring a first branch right towards a pair of gates above, contour on until it

swings slightly up to immediately fork. Take the broad green way rising more to the right, curving to a wall corner. Don't enter the island field but ascend to a gate to the right, from where the hollowed Pannierman's Causeway continues up alongside a hedge. Continue beyond this across heather moor to a gate in a fence opposite.

3. Now just a path, it bears left through diminishing moor to the far corner, merging into a broader green path just short of a bridle-gate. This admits to a walled way running to a gate back onto moorland, with the side valley you are about to cross ahead.

4. Cross a grassy track just a few strides in front onto a thin path slanting right, down through scant heather to a wall. A fence takes over, and a bridle–gate in it sends a thin path along to another gate. An improved path heads into trees, becoming slightly hollowed with a wall to the left. This drops to a ford/stepping-stones on the beck. Rise away with a sidestream to a gate, then ascend the field towards Rosedale Intake.

5. Pass through a gate alongside the house: ignoring the drive heading away, take a broad green path rising straight onto the moor. It eases out to reach a slightly staggered path crossroads at a tiny stream. Go straight across on a thinner, level path, still slightly rising towards the brow with evidence of a stone causeway. Swinging further left in front of a moister section, a sustained length of causeway is enjoyed before reverting to moister terrain: finally leveling out it merges into a moorland road. Go briefly left on the verge to just short of a bridge, and leave by the broad Lord's Turnpike track doubling sharply back right. To the left is the valley of Clitherbeck beneath Danby Beacon.

6. This track runs infallibly across the flat moor, all the way down to an outer wall corner. Bear right to a junction with firmer tracks, and take that straight ahead. This drops quickly down to a gate off the moor. A good track continues down to merge onto the road on the edge of the village, with the crossroads to the right.

8 GLAISDALE

GLAISDALE IS A SCATTERED VILLAGE SPREADING FROM ITS LITTLE RAILWAY STATION BY BEGGAR'S BRIDGE ON THE ESK (VISITED IN WALK 9) UP TO THE EDGE OF GLAISDALE RIGG. AT THE FOOT OF ITS OWN SIDE VALLEY, GLAISDALE BOASTS LOVELY WOODS AND ROLLING MOORS ON ITS DOORSTEP.

Though peaceful enough today, it was a scene of great activity when caught up in the iron ore mining boom of the 19th century. Both the Anglers Rest (which had a temporary name change to relate to the nearby 'Three Blast Furnaces') and the Mitre Tavern which overlooked the green are relatively recent pub casualties, leaving just the Arncliffe Arms to slake thirsts. There is also a Post Office/shop and a butcher.

The valley of Glaisdale was once an important trading route, with several farm names reflecting more distant place-names, including York and London. The Monks' Trod was used by ponies laden with goods when its surface would have been far superior to that of the road. Two troughs standing beneath the causey would have provided water for the ponies.

Glaisdale Rigg is a classic example of a moorland ridge dividing two side valleys – in this case Great Fryup Dale to the west and Glaisdale – that descend in very regular intervals north into Eskdale from the central upland dome of the National Park. The 'road' that you use to descend is also typical of old routes of which many have happily escaped tarmac 'improvement'. It offers superb views not only over the valley of Glaisdale but also Eskdale itself, with further moorland skylines to the north across it.

THE BASICS

Distance: 3½ miles / 5.5km

Gradient: Modest uphill sections

Severity: Generally easy walking

Approx. time to walk: 2½ hours

Stiles: None

Maps: OS Landranger 94 (Whitby); Explorer OL27 (North York Moors Eastern area)

Path description: Largely good moorland paths and tracks

Start Point: Glaisdale village centre (GR NZ 775054)

Parking: Roadside parking near war memorial crossroads (PC YO21 2PN)

Dog friendly: Moorland, dogs preferably on leads

Public toilets: None

Nearest food: Pub near start

8 GLAISDALE WALK

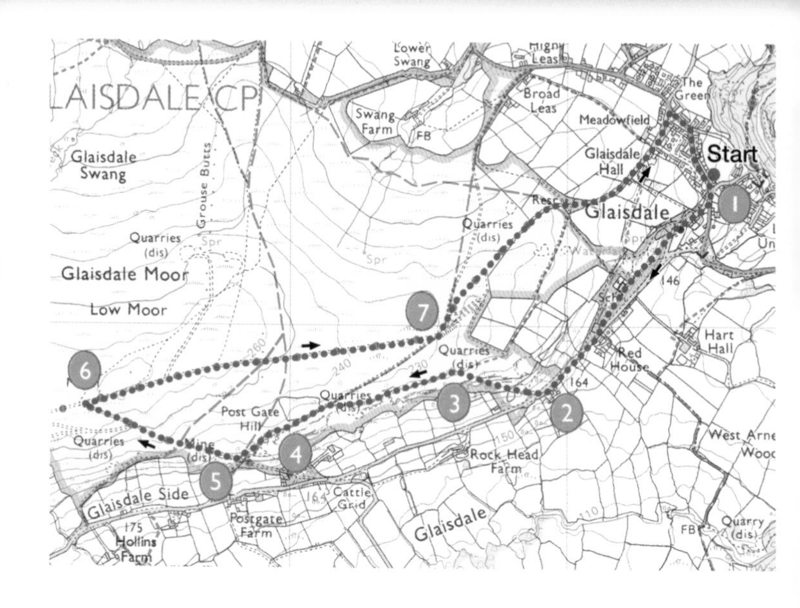

THE ROUTE

1. From the small green by the war memorial and phone box, turn briefly along the side road into Glaisdale. Opposite St Thomas's church gate take a path on the right, running a grassy course across bracken slopes to pass along the front of the school. Continue along the short drive which drops back to the road. Advance on here a short while, with the immediate company of the Monks' Trod stone causeway.

2. As the slopes above open out when the wall climbs away, take an inviting path right shortly after the causeway disappears. This slants up to a gate in a fence just by a wall corner, then continues up the bracken flank. Soon reaching a fork, take the upper one which continues the slant up as a super green path. Before long it arrives at a crossroads with a broader, level way just short of the top of the pull.

3. Turn left on this for a super, near level stride along the flank of the moor. Fine views look out over Glaisdale's own side valley from these colourful moorland flanks. Above a second, larger quarry rim, fork right to the corner of an island pasture used by equestrians at Post Gate Hill. Here you join the broad, grassy track of a tramway built to serve the stone quarries just encountered.

4. Bear left here on this track for a level stroll, quickly passing above the rim of yet another old quarry draped in gorse. Ignoring a branch up to the right the track drops slightly to a fork: go straight ahead to drop quickly through gorse to meet a broader track at a stone-arched bridge. This was connected with an ironstone mine that briefly operated here in the 1870s.

5. Turn right up the broad track, maintaining a steady rise (and ignoring a lesser left fork) to meet the unmistakable course of the unsurfaced Glaisdale Rigg road.

6. All that remains is turn down this to follow it back to the village, ignoring all lesser turnings. An initially largely level section includes the faintest of rises, where twenty paces to the left, just before the brow is a 1967 memorial to someone who "loved the moors", which has curiously even found its way onto the map. Beyond this the road drops very gently down across Glaisdale Low Moor.

7. At a kink amid gorse bushes, the embankment of the former tramway you walked earlier comes in from the right. Around the corner behind it you pass an attractive reedy pool. The road ultimately leaves the still heathery moor at a gate at a lanehead. Simply follow this narrow lane down to Glaisdale Hall Farm, and beyond that it meets the road at a triangular green at the head of the village, going right to finish down the main street.

9 EGTON BRIDGE

In the heart of Eskdale, Egton Bridge and Glaisdale are but two of a whole string of villages served by the splendidly scenic Esk Valley line, a remarkable survivor running a sinuous cul-de-sac course from Middlesbrough to Whitby. How this escaped the Beeching axe of the 1960s still defies logic.

Egton Bridge is a fascinating place, embowered in greenery in a lovely corner of Eskdale. It was the birthplace of Nicholas Postgate, 'Martyr of the Moors', who spent many post-Reformation decades working in this strongly Catholic district. Apprehended in 1679 as an old priest of 82, he was hanged, drawn and quartered at York. His memory is perpetuated by a pub, and his faith by St Hedda's church, famed for its bas-relief panels of scenes from the life of Christ: inside are relics of Father Postgate. Further interest is found in a celebrated Gooseberry Show, held every August for two centuries.

Beggar's Bridge at Glaisdale dates from 1619, a graceful packhorse bridge sat beneath a long, low railway viaduct and also alongside a very bland modern road bridge. It was supposedly built by Tom Ferris, originally a poor local farming lad whose sweetheart Agnes lived on the other bank. Improving his modest beginnings he sailed with Sir Francis Drake, becoming a wealthy and respected figure who became Mayor of Hull, married his Agnes and paid for the beautiful bridge. Just past Glaisdale's railway station is its one surviving pub, the Arncliffe Arms, while the bulk of the village further west features in Walk 8.

The centuries-old pannierway through East Arnecliff Wood is one of the best-known examples of countless such trade routes that criss-crossed Eskdale. Like this, many feature stone flagged surfaces, important in keeping the route passable for packhorses in unfavourable weather conditions. The high-level path largely avoids the steep drop to the river, though it can occasionally be glimpsed.

THE BASICS

Distance: 3¼ miles / 5.25km

Gradient: Only gentle uphill sections

Severity: Easy walking

Approx. time to walk: 2½ hours

Stiles: Five

Maps: OS Landranger 94 (Whitby); Explorer OL27 (North York Moors Eastern area)

Path description: Woodland and field paths

Start Point: Egton Bridge village centre (GR NZ 804052)

Parking: Car park (PC YO21 1UX)

Dog friendly: Sheep pastures, dogs preferably on leads, make sure they can manage the stiles

Public toilets: At start

Nearest food: Pubs at start and pub at Glaisdale mid-walk

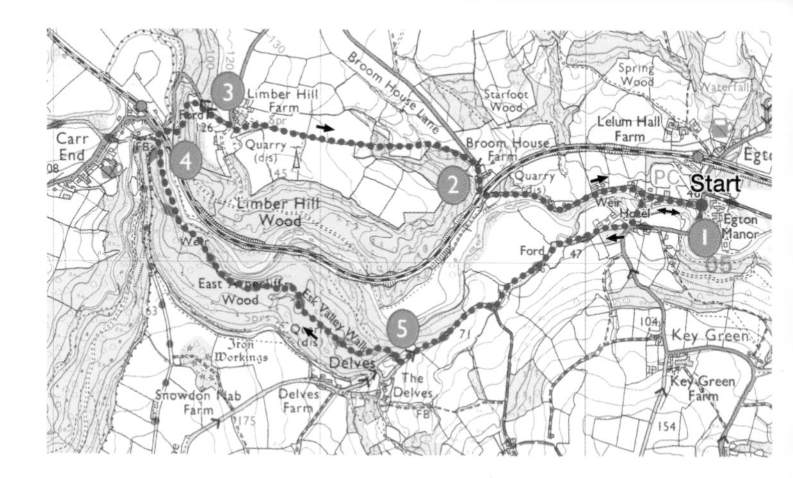

THE ROUTE

1. Leave by the Glaisdale road heading west from the junction below the church, passing the WCs. Leaving the village a nice section of river is enjoyed, then the road runs into woodland before rising away beneath a railway bridge.

2. After a short pull past Broom House take a bridle-gate on the left as the trees end, and head away outside the wood. At the end drop down with a track to a ford/footbridge on a tiny stream, then swing right with that track, briefly, before bearing left up to a stile into trees. A little path climbs directly away, soon leveling out and bearing left to another stile back out. Head away along the hedgeside to a corner stile at the end. Joining a grass track from the tall mast on the left, head for Limber Hill Farm ahead. Before it however, bear left to a tapering corner before the barns. Pass through a gate and along to a drive which runs the few paces right out onto a hairpin bend of the road on Limber Hill.

3. Turn briefly downhill, then from a stile on the left cross to another into the wood just ahead. A good little path slants left down through the trees, easing out to cross a track and down the few steps further to emerge at Beggar's Bridge at Glaisdale.

4. Cross the old bridge, and immediately past the viaduct take a footbridge alongside a setted ford on Glaisdale Beck to enter East Arnecliff Wood. Take the steps directly in front, up to a slanting path which rises briefly left before heading into the wood. The initial section has good river scenery, then climbs away on a prolonged paved section. A gentler, broader conclusion leads out onto a back road at Delves.

5. Turn left down the quiet lane with nice views over the side valley of Egton Grange, and across the main valley to the red roofs of Egton on the slopes beyond. The road enjoys the company of Butter Beck in surroundings that are almost entirely woodland. The beck is crossed at a footbridge/ford, and a pleasant level stroll leads to Egton Bridge. At a T-junction just past the Horseshoe Hotel, go down steps to the river, and a short path runs downstream to dependable stepping-stones. These break their journey at a wooded islet, giving a misleading impression of having already reached the opposite bank. Up onto the road, turn right to retrace opening steps back to the start. If the river should be in spate, avoid the stepping-stones by remaining on the road to the bridge over the Esk.

THIS EASY WALK EXPLORES THE SIDE VALLEY OF THE MURK ESK, BRIMFUL WITH INTEREST AND WITH A STRONG RAILWAY THEME.

Grosmont (pronounced Grow-mont) is a pleasant village at the foot of numerous steep roads. Dominated in the 19th century by ironstone mining (of which scars remain), there is less to see of earlier times, when, as Growmond, it supported an abbey of the little known Grantimontine order: Priory Farm occupies the site. Much earlier still, a Roman fort existed in the neighbourhood. Today railways take centre stage, for here the Esk Valley Line meets the preserved North Yorkshire Moors Railway, each with its own station. Suitably located alongside the level crossing is the Station Tavern, as well as tearooms, shop and bookshop.

The railway line between Pickering and Grosmont was originally part of the Whitby & Pickering Railway, completed in 1836 as a horse-drawn tramway. A decade later it was improved to take steam locomotives. At Beck Hole a steep incline climbed to Goathland, but its deficiencies brought about the construction of a deviation line running between Grosmont and Goathland. Opened in 1865, the replacement track improved the gradient by beginning its climb much earlier. The abandoned line now serves as this footpath. A century later the entire Grosmont-Pickering section was closed, only to be saved by enthusiasts and re-opened, initially to Goathland, in 1973.

Beck Hole exudes character, a sleepy hamlet in an enchanting setting. The Birch Hall Inn is quite simply a gem, with service by way of a small hatch: also doubling as a small shop, this is a time warp but not a museum! Lazily smoking chimneys on red roofs, ducks, sheep, a quoits pitch on the green and even an oil painting for an inn sign - and it is in a hole, too - enjoy! The 1865 re-alignment of the railway left Beck Hole as a very early station casualty, though a plaque on its site records a temporary re-awakening in 1908.

Formed by the confluence of West and Eller Becks at Beck Hole, the Murk Esk is the largest of the Esk's many tributaries. Encountered in curious isolation near the start of the walk, the terraces of Esk Valley housed workers in the ironstone mines, while a former chapel stands to the right.

THE BASICS

Distance: 4¾ miles / 7.5km

Gradient: Modest uphill section midway

Severity: Generally easy walking

Approx. time to walk: 3 to 3½ hours

Stiles: Five

Maps: OS Landranger 94 (Whitby); Explorer OL27 (North York Moors Eastern area)

Path description: Old railway, woodland and field paths

Start Point: Grosmont village centre (GR NZ 827052)

Parking: Two car parks (PC YO22 5PA)

Dog friendly: Dogs preferably on leads, make sure they can manage the stiles

Public toilets: At start

Nearest food: Pub and cafes at start; Pub at Beck Hole mid-walk

THE ROUTE

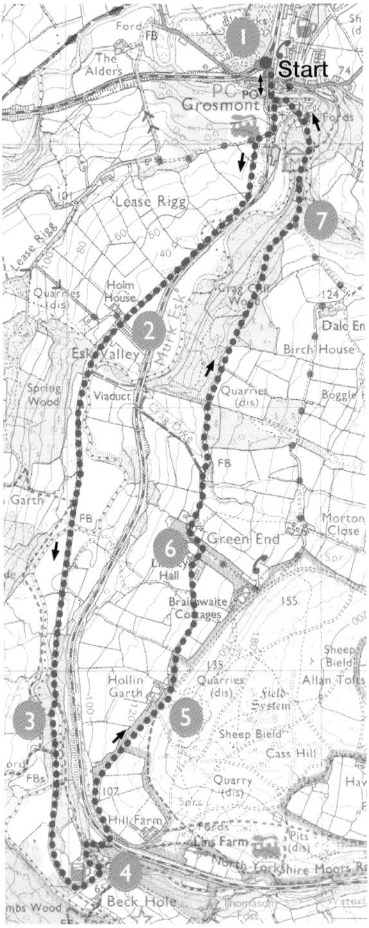

1. Leave Grosmont on a surfaced path by the level crossing on the east side of the NYMR, opposite the signal box. It crosses the Murk Esk on a footbridge parallel with the railway bridge, then forks at the old school tearoom. That straight ahead goes under the tunnel to railway sheds, but your way forks left, slanting up to St Matthew's church. Rising to a gate at the top, turn right to climb a little to a seat with views over the village. Here turn off through a gate on the left, and an enclosed path runs past a viewing platform for the sheds and down to run parallel with the line. Soon a gate gives access to the track of the old line, and resume, parallel with the present line to the houses at Esk Valley.

2. Advance through a gate ahead, and the old line's improved track runs through the Murk Esk's woodland. Beyond a cottage the river is crossed by a footbridge on old railway supports, continuing on and into woodland where another footbridge re-crosses the river alongside a former rail bridge.

3. Continue again through woodland, re-crossing the river on an original rail bridge. A footbridge is reached on inflowing Eller Beck at the site of Beck Hole station. Ignore the bridge and leave the old railway by turning left on a broad beckside path, emerging via a gate into Beck Hole.

4. While the pub is to the right over the bridge, the onward route is left along the road, quickly winding steeply up out of the hamlet. Crossing a railway bridge at the top, keep left along the road opening out onto moorland. Quickly reaching Hollin Garth, take a gate on the left after the farm.

5. Your faint way passes through a bridle-gate followed by a slab bridge and another gate. With a hedge on your left, head for a farm ahead. After the end gate merge into a farm track running through the farmyard out onto an access road. Go briefly left to its demise at Green End.

6. From a gate between houses on the right, cross a small enclosure to a gate/stile ahead. Advance on to become enclosed by hedgerows, a stone causeway easing a moist section. Emerging at a gate, fork right down a grassy path into trees, crossing a bridge and heading away. At the end a field top is crossed to a stile back into woodland. However, the path curves up to a stile straight back out, to run along a field bottom above the wood. After a midway stile, a footbridge at the far end puts you into Crag Cliff Wood. A splendid path heads away, and after a very brief rise it steadily loses height encountering sections of causeway. These lead to a gate out of the wood, and remain in place to point left down the field onto an access road.

7. Turn down this, back into woodland high above the river. Approaching a ford bear left to a footbridge on the Murk Esk, and an enclosed path rises past a burial ground to emerge by the church. Stiles provide a short-cut through the churchyard to rejoin the walk's opening minutes.

11 MAY BECK

THE HAMLET OF LITTLEBECK OCCUPIES A SYLVAN SETTING DEEP IN ITS WOODED VALLEY. FEATURES INCLUDE A FORMER CORNMILL AND A SURVIVING METHODIST CHAPEL OF 1890. ALONGSIDE THE FOOTBRIDGE IS A FORMER WORKSHOP OF THE 'GNOME MAN', A WOODCARVER OF GREAT RENOWN. THOMAS WHITTAKER WORKED ONLY IN OAK, AND ALL HIS CARVINGS BORE A GNOME. HE LIVED AT THE COTTAGE AT THE IMMEDIATE ROAD BEND JUST ABOVE THE BRIDGE UNTIL HIS DEATH IN 1991.

Little Beck Wood is in the hands of Yorkshire Wildlife Trust, and is a beautiful habitat for a rich variety of plant life and wildlife. Though hard to believe today, this was the site of an extensive alum quarry largely active in the 18th century. The Hermitage is quite a curiosity, a shelter hewn out of a solid boulder, with enough room inside for a sizeable group. It was the late 18th century idea of one George Chubb. Its adjacent viewing platform reveals the great depth of this wooded valley. Atop the boulder and easily missed are a pair of 'wishing chairs' also carved from the rocks. Up above is Newton House, built as an 18th century shooting lodge.

Falling Foss is the highlight of the walk, a beautiful waterfall in a glorious setting, and very much a place to linger. Alongside is Midge Hall with its delightful tea garden. Foss Farm was once a hostelry on an old limers' trading road, bringing lime from quarries at Lockton further south to farms near Whitby, where it would be spread on the fields to reduce acidity of the soil. The environs of the old farm enjoy some big views over the Littlebeck valley.

THE BASICS

Distance: 5 miles / 8km

Gradient: Only modest uphill sections

Severity: Generally easy walking

Approx. time to walk: 3 to 3½ hours

Stiles: None

Maps: OS Landranger 94 (Whitby); Explorer OL27 (North York Moors Eastern area)

Path description: Woodland and field paths

Start Point: May Beck (GR NZ 892024)

Parking: Forestry Commission car park off B1416 at Red Gate (PC YO22 5JE)

Dog friendly: Sheep pastures and woodland, dogs preferably on leads

Public toilets: None

Nearest food: Hawsker or Fylingthorpe

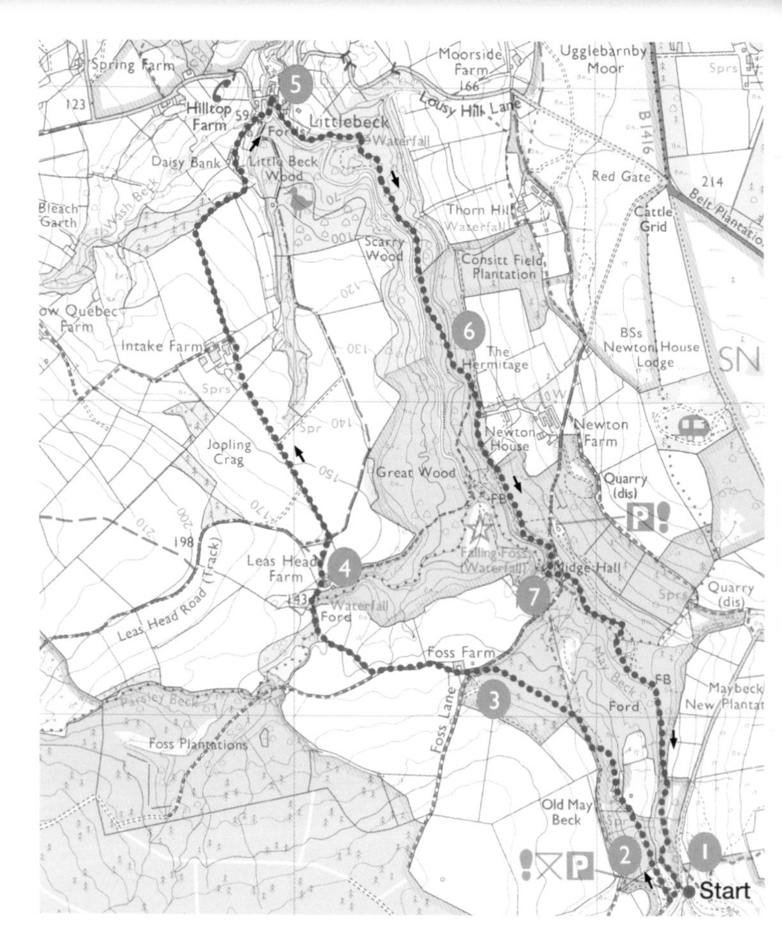

THE ROUTE

1. Don't re-cross the bridge but leave the car park by an access road rising away, and at once turn right on a more inviting cart track. This runs to a gate/stile into woodland, then slants up to the forlorn farm at Old May Beck.

2. Just beyond it a grassy way runs into trees, quickly curving up to the left and faltering before meeting a level path. Just to the left however, a better, sunken green way rises to meet a good path at the top. Turn right, running on to quickly start a gentle descent: just as the field above gives way to dense woodland, ignore the appreciable descent ahead and instead take a less obvious left fork. This contours across into dark forest. For a few minutes the now broad path contours through the sloping wood, at the end swinging left to run up the wood edge parallel with an enclosed cart track. Just a little higher a different cart track

is joined: go right the few strides to meet the other track in front of the barns that were Foss Farm.

3. Go left on the track past the barns to a bridle-gate at the end of the paddock. An enclosed track heads away, soon arriving at a path junction. Turn right through the gate, a better grassy track descending the fieldside to a streamlet and then up to the brow. Continue along the field edge, meeting Parsley Beck and dropping right outside its trees to bridge it in the corner. Through the gate behind, the track runs briefly through trees towards Leas Head Farm.

4. Without entering take a bridle-gate to the left, and slant right up the sloping field. Meeting the access track, ascend it to a gate in the top right corner. Now simply follow the farm drive away, passing Intake Farm to become fully surfaced and down into Littlebeck.

5. Turn right, and over footbridge or ford climb the road only as far as the second bend, with a kissing-gate on the right back into Little Beck Wood. A good path heads upstream, briefly diverted from Little Beck by a waterfall on a tributary, then quickly climbing over a spoil heap. The reserve is left at a gateway in an old wall. Before long the path climbs steeply, culminating in stone steps up to The Hermitage boulder.

6. Leave by the upper, level path, and when this soon forks take the main, right branch slanting gently down. Quickly joined by a wall from the left, the path runs grandly on to a fork: go right through an old wall-gap. The path slants slightly then runs a well-made course above a steep drop and beneath a small crag. Absorbing another path, it curves down to Falling Foss, and you soon arrive at a viewpoint above the waterfall, with Midge Hall tea garden alongside.

7. From the nearby footbridge take the path up to a farm road and turn left over the stone-arched bridge. Turn immediately right and resume upstream on a path above the opposite bank. After a bridle-gate an area of more scattered trees leads back to May Beck's bridge.

12 STAITHES

STAITHES IS A FISHING PORT ONCE OF GREAT IMPORTANCE, AND LIKE ROBIN HOOD'S BAY IS A FORMER SMUGGLING CENTRE. DESCENDING TOWARDS THE SEAFRONT ITS BUILDINGS CLUSTER INTO LITTLE SPACE, EITHER PERCHED ABOVE THE DEEP-CUT STAITHES BECK OR FACING THE SMALL HARBOUR. IT IS THE SEA THAT IS LINKED WITH EVERY ASPECT OF LOCAL LIFE, AND STAITHES HAS SEEN ITS SHARE OF SAVAGE STORMS. THERE ARE PUBS, SHOPS, A GALLERY AND EATERIES.

It was at Staithes that James Cook earned his first wages serving in a shop, and a story relates how a south-sea coin he took in inspired him to begin his life of adventure. There is an absorbing Captain Cook & Staithes Heritage Centre and an annual arts festival.

The deep rift of Staithes Beck features a buttress of the Whitby, Redcar & Middlesbrough Union Railway, opened in 1883 and closed in 1958: the iron viaduct was demolished in 1960.

Port Mulgrave is a fascinating place, with its mini harbour separated from the hamlet by 300ft of rough slopes. The tiny port was constructed in the 1850s when ironstone mining was in full swing, with the ore shipped up the coast to ironworks on Tyneside. During World War Two the Royal Engineers blew up the harbour wall to deter enemy invasion, and the scene today is of near dereliction: just a short, collapsed section of pier survives beside the old harbour, while a handful of small boats are drawn up in front of an absorbing cluster of fishermens' shacks.

Hinderwell village clings doggedly to the main road through it. St Hilda's church dates from 1773 and within its churchyard is an ancient well, said to have been blessed by Hilda, who was Abbess of Whitby in the 7th century – hence the name of the village. Further left along the street are pubs, shops and tearoom.

The hamlet of Dalehouse shelters the welcoming Fox & Hounds pub, and in its environs several becks merge to form the short-lived Staithes Beck. For a quick finish simply continue straight up the road, turning briefly right on the main road to the Staithes Lane junction. Looming to the north, Boulby potash mine is a modern addition whose thousands of feet of tunnels would be fine if they didn't require the unsightly surface works!

THE BASICS

Distance: 5 miles / 8km

Gradient: Only modest uphill sections

Severity: Generally easy walking

Approx. time to walk: 3 to 3½ hours

Stiles: Six

Maps: OS Landranger 94 (Whitby); Explorer OL27 (North York Moors Eastern area)

Path description: Woodland, field and coastal paths

Start Point: Staithes village (GR NZ 780184)

Parking: Bank Top car park at top of village (PC TS13 5AD)

Dog friendly: Dogs preferably on leads, make sure they can manage the stiles

Public toilets: At start

Nearest food: Pubs and café at start, Port Mulgrave, and Hinderwell, pub at Dalehouse

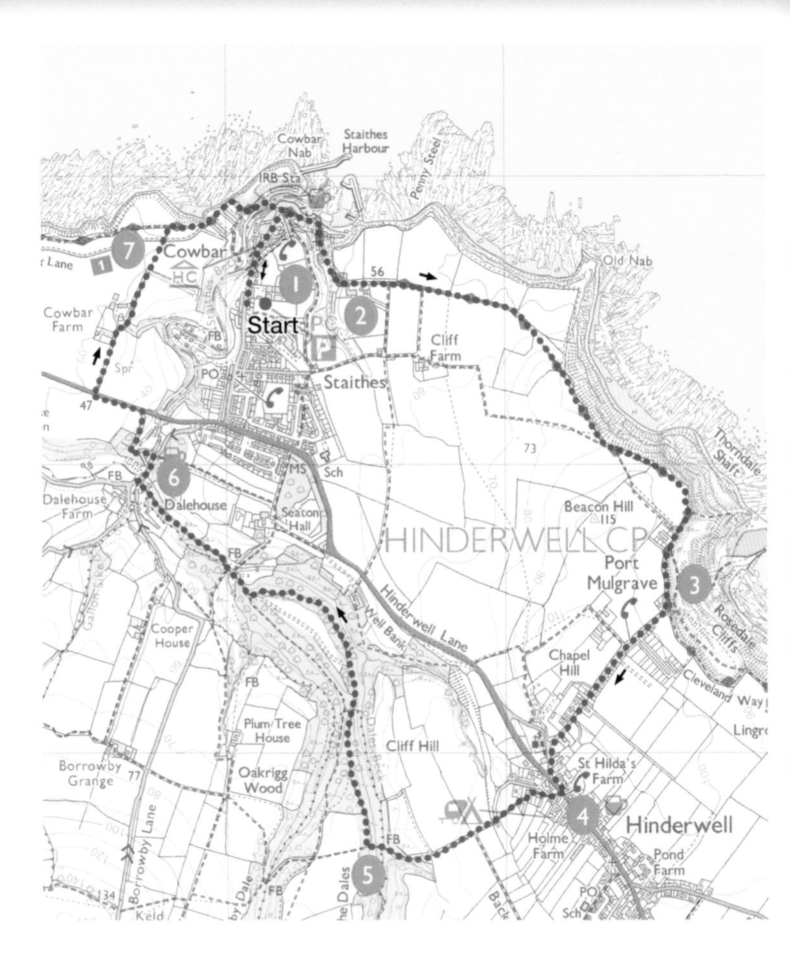

THE ROUTE

1. From the car park turn down the main street towards the seafront. Keep on towards the end and depart by Church Street climbing behind the Cod & Lobster pub. At the road's demise a path takes over, going left at a fork to rise to Fullwood Farm.

2. Pass left of the buildings onto a driveway, briefly, then advance straight on an enclosed path. This opens out to cross a long fieldside, rising at the end to a bridle-gate. Continue rising to a fence above the cliffs, with Runswick Bay and Kettle Ness appearing. Turning right up to a corner bridle-gate, the clifftop path soon arrives at an access road at Port Mulgrave. Remain on it as it swings inland.

3. Passing the Ship Inn a T-junction is reached at Hinderwell church. A raised footway runs left to the main road.

4. Go briefly left to turn down Porret Lane opposite, noting a thatched cottage. After a former chapel a narrow path bears left by the front of a terrace of houses. This unlikely way swings left at the end, running as a snicket to emerge onto a lane. Cross straight over and down an enclosed path onto another lane alongside a house. Advance straight on a track ahead, soon crossing the old railway. When it swings sharply left, take a stile in front and continue along a lesser, enclosed way. Through a stile at the end a path drops right to a stile into trees, then slants down to a footbridge over Dales Beck in Borrowby Dale.

5. Across, a stepped path climbs to a small gate out of the trees: turn right along the field edge to re-enter trees at a corner stile. Go left, an excellent woodland path tracing the crest of Oak Rigg. Further along it drops left off the ridge to run beneath it, to a gate into a clearing. With scrub to both sides a green path continues through Oakridge Nature Reserve, ultimately dropping as a firmer track onto an access road amid caravans. Cross a bridge in front, and advance straight on to merge with another access road out to Dalehouse.

6. Turn right to the pub where you go left to an abrupt road-end at Dalehouse Bridge. Across it turn right, doubling back up this old road onto the A174. Across, use the verge to rise briefly left. Just past a boundary sign escape right along Cowbar Farm drive. Just short of the house a stile takes the path right, round a fenceside out into a field. Bear left alongside a fence past the house and along to a railway underpass. Keep straight on across a field to a kissing-gate onto Cowbar Lane.

7. Just ahead is the old road. Bear right to join it at a fence gap, and turn right to the houses at Cowbar. The road drops past terraces with awesome cliff views on your left, and down past further cottages to the bottom, with the lifeboat station ahead beneath Cowbar Nab. Take the footbridge over Staithes Beck and up a little alley onto the main street.

13 RUNSWICK BAY

RUNSWICK IS A PLACE OF CONTRASTS: WHILE RUNSWICK BANK TOP IS QUITE ORDINARY, ITS LOWER HALF OF RUNSWICK BAY PRESENTS A STUNNING SCENE OF BRIGHT COTTAGES GROUPED IN TOTAL DISARRAY IN THE SHADOW OF THE CLIFF. IN AMONGST IS THE ROYAL HOTEL, WHILE THE LAST HOUSE AT THE END IS THATCHED. THIS DELECTABLE CORNER BOASTS AN ENVIABLE POSITION, FACING SOUTH ACROSS ITS BAY. LABYRINTHINE PATHS WEAVE IN BETWEEN THE DWELLINGS: ONCE FISHERMEN'S HOMES, MANY ARE NOW HOLIDAY HOMES. YOU WILL EXPERIENCE THIS AT THE END.

The Whitby, Redcar & Middlesbrough Union Railway - better known as the Whitby-Loftus line – opened in 1883 and closed in 1958, and ran a dramatic coastal journey that had caused construction and subsequent maintenance headaches. The line was re-opened in the 1970s from Saltburn as far as Boulby, purely as a mineral line serving the potash mine above Staithes. The old railway is a permissive path courtesy of the Mulgrave Estate.

Kettleness is a tiny community that was once larger, for back in 1829 a previous hamlet fell victim to the North Sea. Nearby is the site of a Roman signal station. Alum works here were the last in the district to close in 1871. Beyond Kettleness was a 300-yard long rail tunnel, beyond which it ran across the cliff of Seaveybog Hill towards the much longer Sandsend Tunnel.

Approaching Kettleness, alongside the old line are the remains of Kettleness Mines, with spoil heaps and a former tramway from early 20th century ironstone mining. Entering the hamlet, the well-preserved old station and platforms, now a scout base, stand just to the left. Visible just up the road is a former chapel that began in 1872 as the Mission church of St John the Baptist.

As you finally gain the shore at Hob Holes near the end of the walk, these intriguingly named small caves recall that a hob was a goblin-like character peculiar to the region: some were mischievous, others had healing powers.

THE BASICS

Distance: 5¼ miles / 8.5km

Gradient: One steep road section at end

Severity: Generally easy walking

Approx. time to walk: 3 to 3½ hours

Stiles: None

Maps: OS Landranger 94 (Whitby); Explorer OL27 (North York Moors Eastern area)

Path description: Old railway and coastal paths

Start Point: Runswick Bank Top (GR NZ 806161)

Parking: Car park just beyond Runswick Bay Hotel (PC TS13 5RT)

Dog friendly: Dogs preferably on leads

Public toilets: None

Nearest food: Pub at start

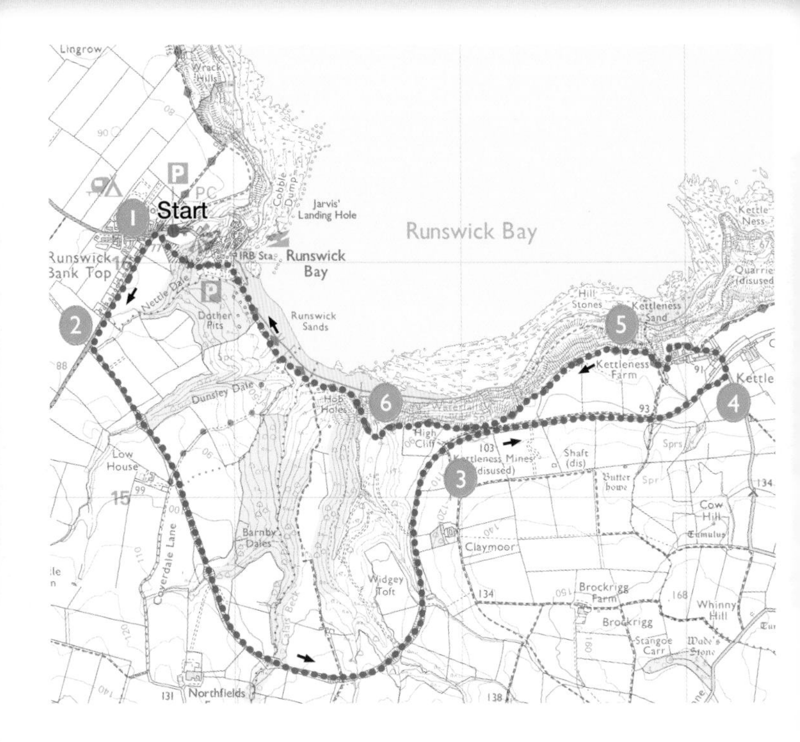

THE ROUTE

1. From the Runswick Bay Hotel, head away from the coast along Ellerby Lane opposite. Leaving the houses behind it makes a slight dip, where you will find the almost hidden course of an old railway branching off left.

2. A delightful path follows it through undergrowth, soon broadening into a cart track leading to a lone cottage at Ellerby Crossing. The way resumes as a broad track, and with nice open views makes an enormous sweep around the side valley of Barnby Dales to come back out the other side. Increasing views look back over Runswick Bay to the village backed by Boulby Cliff and potash mine.

3. Reaching an estate gate, one on the left sends a short-cut down to the return route at a gate below. Note also that from a kissing-gate just below, a public footpath takes a parallel route beneath the old line, rejoining it further along for the last short section to Kettleness. Simply remain on the old line, passing mining remains as it curves left to approach the houses at Kettleness. As the old line runs on to the former station, your track runs to a gate onto the hamlet's access road.

4. Turn left on the short-lived road down to an area of unkempt greens. Keep on to the end and bear right of Kettleness Farm out above the coastline. The path runs outside the grounds and back at the other side to bear right as a briefly enclosed track past a final cottage. Emerging into a field, the path bears right and now clings to the headland. Good views look back to Kettle Ness and ahead to Runswick Bay.

5. Regaining a little height, the path passes through a gate just beneath your outward route, then on to a seat marking the start of a steep, stepped descent into undergrowth. A gentler section midway precedes further steps as the path drops into the shale ravine of a trickling stream and down to Runswick Sands at Hob Holes: the final section involves a very modest down-clamber.

6. Simply turn left for the half-mile stroll back to the village, almost at once passing the caves of Hob Holes. Further, you pass a sailing clubhouse and a World War Two pill box that has fallen to the shore. All that remains is a stiff haul up the access road back to Bank Top.

14 ROBIN HOOD'S BAY

ROBIN HOOD'S BAY, WITH THE ADVANTAGES OF AN EXCITING NAME AND EVEN BETTER LOCATION, WILL BE FOUND ON MANY LISTS OF FAVOURITE PLACES. ONCE THE PRESERVE OF FISHERMEN AND SMUGGLERS, IT IS NOW VERY MUCH PART OF THE TOURIST ITINERARY. KNOWN LOCALLY SIMPLY AS BAY TOWN, IT CONSISTS OF A CHAOTIC TUMBLE OF RED-ROOFED BUILDINGS SQUEEZED INTO A NARROW GAP BETWEEN THE CLIFFS.

From the modern extension of housing at the clifftop, the steep main street plunges down to the very shore. On each side are irregularly grouped buildings with absorbing narrow passageways linking near-hidden doorsteps. The street features several pubs, cafes and shops, including second-hand bookshops.

The village has suffered badly from storms, and the Bay Hotel once had a ship driven into it by the savage weather. Some 200 houses have been lost to the sea, though a modern sea wall now ensures more security. Also at the foot of the street is the National Trust's Old Coastguard visitor centre. The bay itself is a geologists' Mecca, with fossils in abundance and a spectacular sweep of flat scars curving round the bay almost like a natural extension of the tide. Since the 1970s this has been the terminus of Wainwright's celebrated Coast to Coast Walk, concluding a journey of almost 200 miles that begins at St Bees on the Irish Sea coast of Cumbria.

Rocket Post Field recalls when the coastguard service would practice firing rockets at the post which replicated the mast of a distressed ship. Fired in earnest, they carried a rope bringing lifesaving equipment, and even a stronger rope that could carry a man. It was in use for much of the 20th century, and a replica still stands.

The Scarborough-Whitby Railway existed from 1885 to 1965, when it was purchased by Scarborough Council to create a magnificent walkers' and cyclists' trail. During Stage 3 the surroundings open out to provide sweeping panoramas from the old line over the outward route to Ravenscar and the Bay, a big seascape.

THE BASICS

Distance: 5 miles / 8km

Gradient: One steep road section at end

Severity: Generally easy walking

Approx. time to walk: 3 to 3½ hours

Stiles: None

Maps: OS Landranger 94 (Whitby); Explorer OL27 (North York Moors Eastern area)

Path description: Old railway and coastal paths

Start Point: Robin Hood's Bay village (GR NZ 950054)

Parking: Station car park (PC YO22 4RA)

Dog friendly: Dogs preferably on leads

Public toilets: At start

Nearest food: Pubs and cafes at start

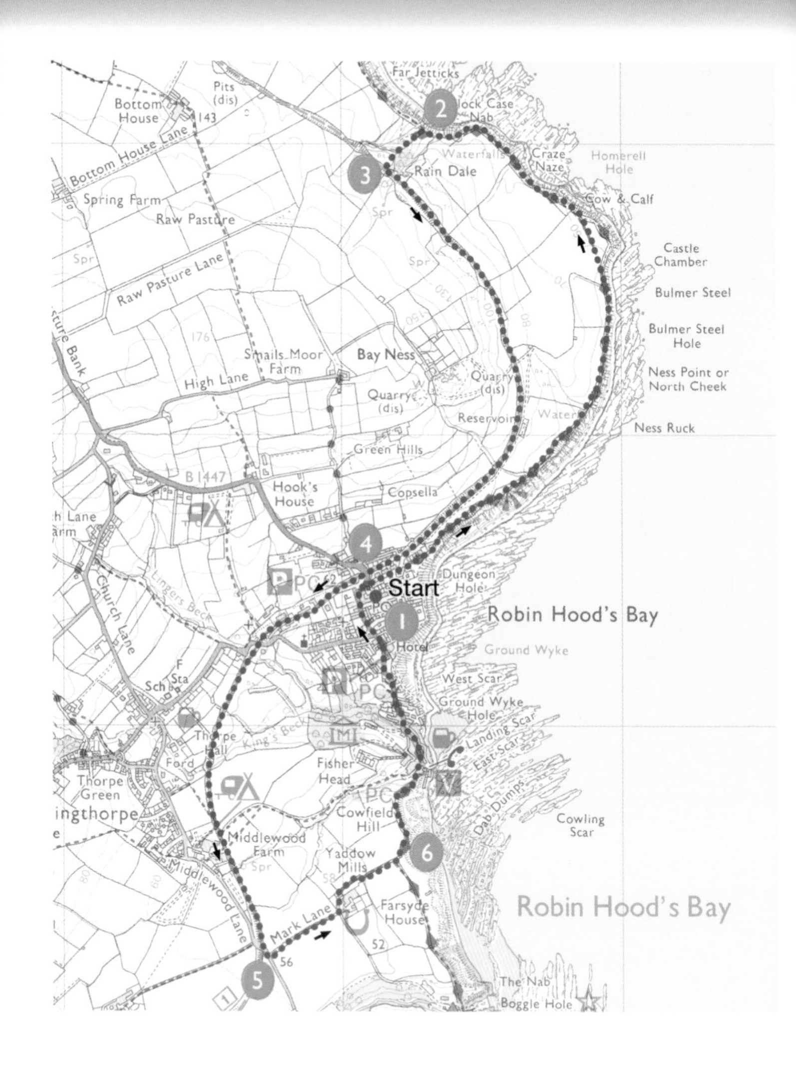

THE ROUTE

1. From the car park entrance cross the road to the Grosvenor Hotel and head along the suburban street of Mount Pleasant North. At the end the ways fork: the Cinder Track (your return route) climbs left, while your Cleveland Way path passes through a gate in front and along the front of houses before emerging into Rocket Post Field. Simply remain on the coastal footpath for about a mile and a half around the headland of Ness Point. Sections on the cliff side of the fence demand caution if young children are in the party, while at other times the path is diverted to the 'safe' side due to landslips. Good views look out over the sea as you pass beneath an old coastguard lookout.

2. With larger cliffs in view ahead, the prize moment comes on gaining the promontory at Clock Case Nab, looking directly ahead to taller cliffs. The path swings left and rises briefly to a gateway. Here at the bracken-filled hollow of Rain Dale you abandon the coastal path as directed by a sign pointing a grassy path left up the wallside. It climbs to pass through gorse at the top and gain the old railway line via a kissing-gate.

3. Turn left, and at the end of the long, gentle decline you are halted by houses, whereupon the way drops left back onto Mount Pleasant North.

4. Returning to the car park pass straight through, past the old station itself and on a path paralleling the access road at the far end. You emerge onto Thorpe Lane just past St Stephen's tall-towered church. Cross and advance briefly on the road, then bear left to rejoin the old railway. Initially an access road, it soon narrows to run pleasantly beneath the small village of Fylingthorpe, which includes the Fylingdales Inn. The line crosses a track at busy Middlewood Farm with its caravan site to quickly meet Middlewood Lane.

5. Here leave the old line and go left a few strides to turn left along cul-de-sac Mark Lane, which quickly ends at Farsyde Stud. The continuing enclosed path runs briefly left of the buildings to emerge into the far end of the yard. Cross to the corner ahead where a bridle-gate sends a delightful enclosed path away, later dropping down to a fieldside to rejoin the Cleveland Way. Turn left, emerging above grassy seaward slopes to be rewarded with a magnificent view of the village and the bay.

6. The flagged path runs on to quickly make a stepped descent. Keeping right at a fork it drops onto the Quarterdeck, then left up and back down further steps to emerge onto the very foot of the village street at the Bay Hotel adjoining the foreshore. You may wish to linger on the beach here before turning left up the street to finish – possibly via some intriguing alleyways.

ROBIN HOOD'S BAY

TO SEA WALL
KING STREET
FOR SALE
Brooke Bond Tea
KING STREET
PEDESTRIAN ACCESS
GR
SAND TOYS

15 WEST AYTON

AYTON IS A BUSTLING LITTLE PLACE, HANDILY PLACED FOR SCARBOROUGH COMMUTERS BUT RETAINING ITS OWN CHARACTER. THE TWIN VILLAGES OF EAST AND WEST AYTON ARE DIVIDED BY THE RIVER DERWENT, BUT LINKED BY THE LONG, GRACEFUL BRIDGE THAT SPANS THE RIVER AND STILL SERVES EASTBOUND TRAFFIC. WEST AYTON HAS THE FORGE VALLEY INN, AND A CASTLE AND OLD MILL BOTH PASSED AT THE END OF THE WALK. HERE ALSO IS A FORMER STATION KNOWN AS 'FORGE VALLEY' ON THE PICKERING-SCARBOROUGH RAILWAY OPENED IN 1882 AND CLOSED IN 1950.

East Ayton boasts the church of St John the Baptist, whose surviving Norman features include the font. Here also are the Denison Arms, a service station shop, Post office, fish-shop and restaurant/tearoom.

The Forge Valley is the name given to a two-mile length of the River Derwent as it forces its way south through a narrow break in the Tabular Hills. This escape into the Vale of Pickering was made at the end of the last Ice Age. The valley is so named because an iron foundry - possibly established by the monks of Rievaulx Abbey - existed here until the late 18th century: the forges were fuelled by charcoal made in these woods. The Forge Valley is a scene of great wooded beauty in a corner of the National Park known more for its blanket of conifers. Of sufficient importance to be a National Nature Reserve, the valley bottom is filled by the untainted river and its parallel road, and all else is rich slopes dominated by ash, oak and the like - a living relic of the wildwoods of ancient times. Also here you encounter Wallis Quarry, site of a form of limestone known as Hambleton Oolite, renowned for its fossil content.

Ayton Castle was the 14th century fortified house of the Evers family, and is raised slightly above the village, commanding a wide view over the Vale of Pickering to the Wolds. It is rare to find such a pele tower so far from the Scottish border, but it was clearly needed as the Scots did indeed raid the original structure on one of their forays south. Alongside is an extensive network of earthworks. Right at the end of the walk, the old mill is a splendid three-storey building of 1843, and it complements a lovely corner where ducks waddle from the water to dabble on the grassy sward.

THE BASICS

Distance: 5 miles / 8km

Gradient: One modest uphill section in woods

Severity: Generally easy walking

Approx. time to walk: 3 to 3½ hours

Stiles: None

Maps: OS Landranger 101 (Scarborough); Explorer OL27 (North York Moors Eastern area)

Path description: Good woodland paths

Start Point: West Ayton village centre (GR SE 987847)

Parking: Start from the bridge between East and West Ayton,

lay-bys on both sides (PC YO13 9JE)

Dog friendly: Sheep pastures, dogs preferably on leads

Public toilets: None

Nearest food: Pub and café at start

THE ROUTE

1. From the bridge on the Derwent turn towards East Ayton, leaving the main road along Castlegate on the left. Almost at once comes a fine view across the river to Ayton Castle. With its useful footway the road leaves the village, passing Ayton Lodge Hotel and descending to a riverside area, now in the Forge Valley proper. Keep on past a bridleway going off right before Whitestone Quarry, and leave at a footpath sign a little way beyond a weir opposite the end of the quarry.

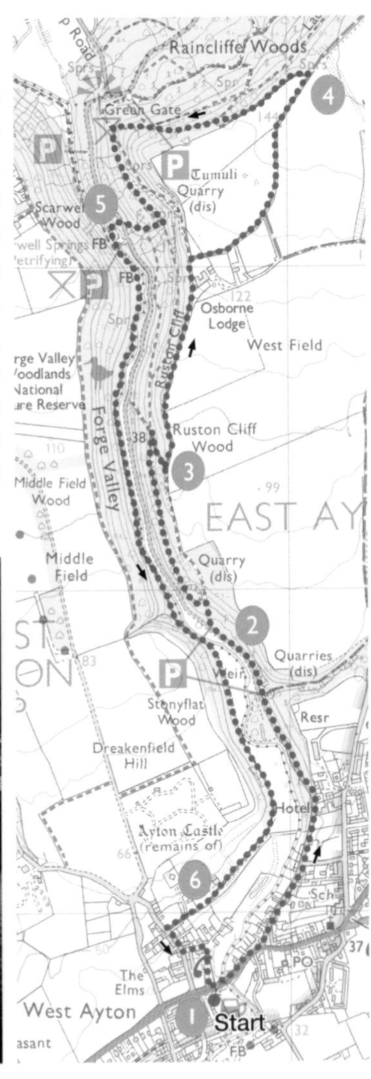

2. A broad path rises away into Ruston Cliff Wood, but is quickly left by a branch rising briefly left, quickly swinging right to arrive beneath the former Wallis Quarry. Beyond it the path broadens to commence a superb, largely level stroll along a terrace at mid height through the wood. This is maintained for a good half-mile until the path suddenly turns to drop away. Here take the upper branch that doubles back right from a few wooden steps, maintaining its slant to quickly arrive at the top of the woods, where turn left.

3. From the wallside the woodland delights are joined by views back across the fields to the Vale of Pickering. Immediately beyond Osborne Lodge, take a break from the woods at a kissing-gate on the right. An enclosed path heads away, and when it opens out simply remain with the right-hand wall which swings left, passing a path junction and continuing to a bridle-gate into Raincliffe Woods.

4. Take the path left along the wood top. After a long quarter-mile, in a slight dip from the fence, two paths drop away right. While a narrow, sunken way doubles back right, yours is that slanting gently right. Descending steadily it drops a little more firmly onto a broader, level path, Lady Mildred's Ride. Turn left on this, quickly descending wooden steps onto a broader way. Turn left, rising a little too quickly run to a fork at a small clearing. While the main one rises left as a uniform climb, your way is the thinner path straight ahead. This runs a level course, broadening and encountering boardwalks before descending wooden steps, soon more steeply right down onto the valley road at a parking area. Turn right to quickly reach a riverside car park.

5. From here a short path runs upstream to a footbridge over the river, from where a well-trodden path turns downstream, clinging to the water's edge as it glides serenely through glorious surrounds. This entire section is along boardwalks to preserve the delicate habitat. Ultimately the river is forsaken at a kissing-gate out of the woods. The path runs along a lengthy fieldside beneath a wooded bank, and just short of the far corner a broader path rises to a gate into a field. A grassy way runs on past the ruinous Ayton Castle.

6. Beyond the castle you emerge via a gate onto a short street. Turn left at the end then left again on Mill Lane, to rejoin the Derwent where the mill-cut emerges from beneath the old mill. The main road is just downstream.

16 SALTERGATE

THE HOLE OF HORCUM IS A FAMOUS FEATURE ALONGSIDE THE BUSY A169, TAKING THE FORM OF AN ENORMOUS BOWL CARVED OUT OF THE MOORS BY GLACIAL ACTION DURING THE END OF THE ICE AGE. THE CAR PARK AT SALTERGATE BANK IS VERY CONVENIENTLY PLACED FOR PASSING TOURISTS TO PULL IN AND SIMPLY CROSS THE ROAD TO SAVOUR THE SPLENDID VIEW. ON THE OTHER SIDE OF THE HOLLOW IS LEVISHAM MOOR, VISITED ON WALK 17 FROM LEVISHAM.

Saltergate's name relates to it being astride a one-time salt traders' route. The landmark Saltersgate Inn (not a mistake, the spellings do differ!) on the road north dates from the mid 17th century, and achieved prominence due to its peat fire reputedly burning for the best part of 200 years. Sadly the pub closed in 2007, though after being purchased in Summer 2016, hopes remain that its doors will one day re-open.

Well seen for much of the walk, but notably above Newgate Brow, is Blakey Topping, highly distinctive if a little meek, at 876ft/267m being no higher than your viewpoint. This relic of the Ice Age is now largely surrounded by forestry, further diminishing its stature. Also looking good from Newgate Brow is the colourful side valley of Long Gill to the left, with a small reservoir at Cargate Spring in its lap.

Malo Cross stands at the foot of Whinny Nab, a hill which it originally graced prior to being restored to its present site in modern times. It was a landmark on the old Whitby-Pickering road, and its prominent inscription is thought to refer to Richard Egerton, Knight. Visitors often leave loose change here, maintaining an ancient tradition when alms for the needy would be left at such locations. Looking north, RAF Fylingdales presents a hugely contrasting moorland landmark. This military monitoring station is a well-known, almost endearing yet not universally welcomed feature of the North York Moors. Its famous 'golf balls' (radomes) were replaced in 1992 by the present, more advanced 'pyramid' structure – also more casually known as the 'sandcastle'.

THE BASICS

Distance: 4¼ miles / 6.75km

Gradient: Negligible

Severity: Generally easy walking

Approx. time to walk: 2½ to 3 hours

Stiles: Two

Maps: OS Landranger 94 (Whitby); Explorer OL27 (North York Moors Eastern area)

Path description: Good tracks and field paths

Start Point: Saltergate Bank on A169 (GR SE 852937)

Parking: National Park car park (PC YO18 7NS)

Dog friendly: Sheep pastures, dogs preferably on leads, make sure they can manage the stiles

Public toilets: None

Nearest food: Pub at Lockton

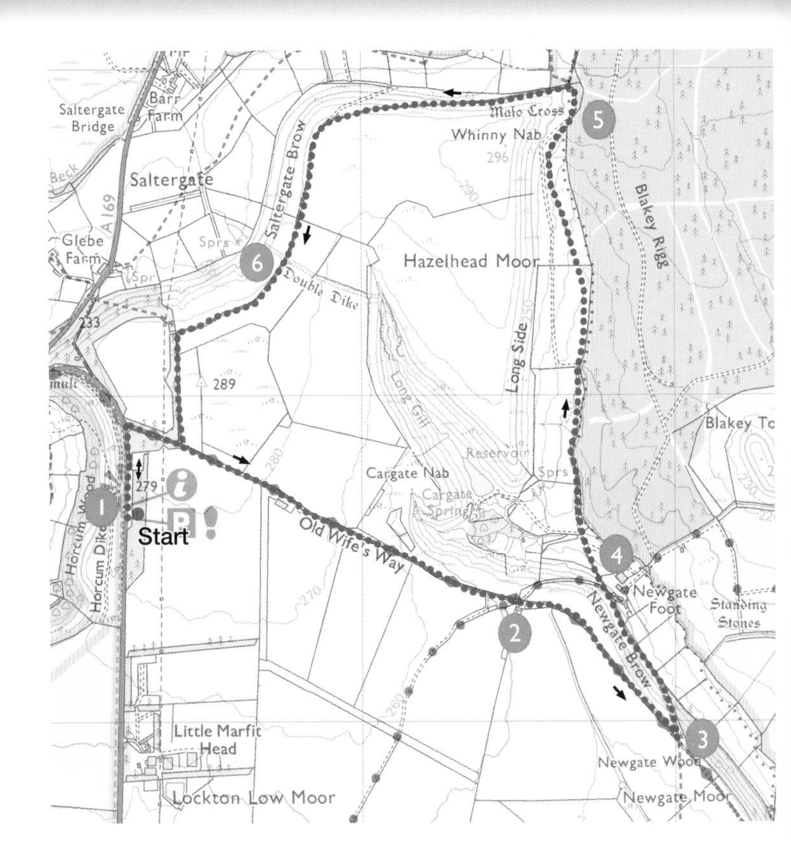

THE ROUTE

1. From the car park cross the main road with care and turn briefly right (north) on a footpath along the road's verge, looking down upon the impressive Hole of Horcum. Before the bend you must re-cross the road in time to turn off along an access road (Old Wife's Way) to the right. This is followed for almost a mile to the point where it commences a steep drop to the farm at Newgate Foot.

2. As the road begins a steep descent, instead bear right along a track past a National Trust sign. Through a gate it runs a super grassy course above the bank of Newgate Brow. Looking back, the 'sandcastle' of RAF Fylingdales sneaks into view.

3. On reaching a stile in the adjacent fence, ignore it but leave the track by taking a couple of strides left to find a path dropping to a stile just below. The path now descends pleasantly in company with the fence, then traces the fence left along the base of the bracken bank to join the drive just above Newgate Foot Farm.

4. Cross to a bridle-gate almost opposite, and head away on a green path swinging left. Quickly turn down to another gate just below, then slant left down the field to a corner gate. A grass track heads away to a gate ahead: the whole of this section runs outside a forest fence, with the bracken-draped slopes of Hazelhead Moor over to the left. Ignoring a track rising left, keep straight on the lower one close by the fence. Through a gate at the end continue along the fenceside, an intermittent trod leading to a stile. A green path heads directly away on a gentle rise through bracken beneath Hazelhead Moor. At a gate a track merges, and you advance along this to immediately reveal Malo Cross just ahead.

5. Leaving the cross, take the broad green path left alongside the fence beneath Whinny Nab. It soon slants gently up the bracken bank to emerge onto the sheep pasture of Hazelhead Moor. It now continues in grand style above Saltergate Brow, running to a gate in a fence. Though the obvious way is on the rim of the colourful bank just below, the actual bridleway maintains a level course, curving around through the hugely prominent ancient earthwork of Double Dyke. Visible below is the white-walled, currently derelict Saltersgate Inn.

6. The grass track runs across the field centre to the trees ahead, where a bridle-gate sends an enclosed path sharply left through the pencil woodland to rejoin the farm road very near the start of the walk. Turn right to finish as you began.

17 LEVISHAM

LEVISHAM IS A GOOD EXAMPLE OF A STREET VILLAGE, A LAYOUT VERY COMMON IN THIS AREA. ITS ATTRACTIVE STONE DWELLINGS STAND WELL BACK FROM THE ROAD, WITH WIDE GRASSY MARGINS. AT ITS HEAD STANDS THE HORSESHOE INN, IN FRONT OF WHICH IS A SMALL GREEN WITH A MAYPOLE, AND THE CHURCH OF ST JOHN THE BAPTIST CLOSE BY. THE VILLAGE STANDS ON THE EDGE OF A BROAD PLATEAU, ITS ONLY ROAD ACCESS BEING FROM LOCKTON VIA THE STEEP VALLEY FLOOR AT LEVISHAM MILL. THE FORMER MILL MAKES A HIGHLY ATTRACTIVE SCENE, WITH DUCKS SPLASHING BY THE BECK, AND A WATERWHEEL STILL IN SITU.

Levisham has its own little station on the North Yorkshire Moors Railway, a mile and a half distant and some 350ft lower in the deep trough of Newton Dale. Steam trains call here midway through their magnificent 18-mile journey between Pickering and Grosmont.

Levisham Moor is a splendid patch of open country, punctured by a number of deep-cut little side valleys locally known as 'griffs': your walk up to Dundale Pond enjoys the colourful charms of Dundale Griff. Dundale Pond is an artificial sheet of water thought to have been created by the monks of Malton Priory to cater for their grazing flocks and herds. Today much impinged on by reeds, it nevertheless makes a very obvious place for a break. The walk's opening section sees Levisham Beck (fresh from departing the Hole of Horcum, visited in Walk 16) flow through a gem of a steep-sided dale sandwiched between highly productive agricultural plateaux. This is a good location to spot an adder on warmer days.

THE BASICS

Distance: 3½ miles / 5.5km

Gradient: One modest uphill section

Severity: Generally easy walking

Approx. time to walk: 2½ hours

Stiles: None

Maps: OS Landranger 94 (Whitby) or Landranger 100 (Malton & Pickering); Explorer OL27 (North York Moors Eastern area)

Path description: Good moorland paths and tracks

Start Point: Levisham village centre (GR SE 833905)

Parking: Roadside parking (PC YO18 7NL)

Dog friendly: moorland, dogs preferably on leads

Public toilets: None

Nearest food: Pub at start

17 LEVISHAM WALK

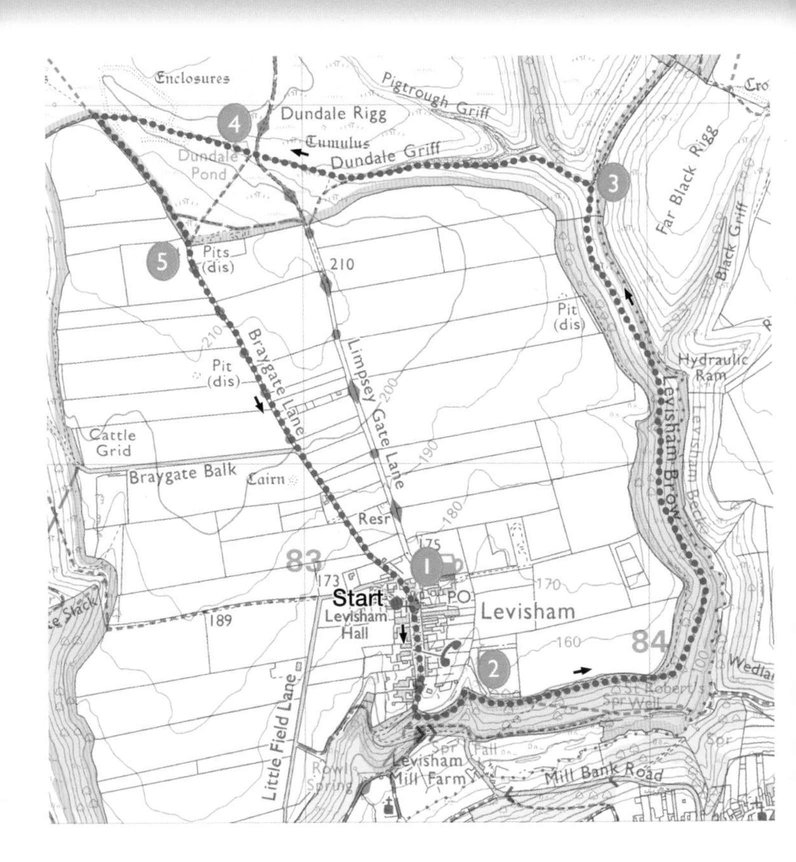

THE ROUTE

1. Leave the village by the road to Lockton and the outside world, but as it leaves the houses to drop through the woods, leave it for a seat on the left. While one path drops directly away, yours runs left to undulate along the top of the steep scrubby slope: at an early stage after a stepped climb, remain on the main, upper path rather than a lesser branch descending right at a fork.

2. At a sharp corner the upper path swings left to run along Levisham Brow, high above Levisham Beck. The super little path eventually slants down a little to run through the trees, which later give way to bracken and scrub as things open out and the path drops closer to the beck. A little beyond a bridle-gate is a guidepost by the beck.

3. Here turn sharp left on a green path up the side of Dundale Griff, a mini-dale likely to be dry. As height is gained heather joins the bracken, while sturdy oaks line the edge of the little ravine. As the going eases on the more open moor, keep right at a fork to run gently along to a busy junction of moorland ways in front of Dundale Pond.

4. Continue straight on the clear path running immediately left of the pond. It shadows the reedy trough of the little feeder stream, then angles up to a brow, with a path crossroads at a wall corner just ahead. Here double back left on the wallside way to arrive at the head of an enclosed lane.

5. Pass through the gate and as Braygate Lane this will lead unfailingly back towards the village, joining a road for the final stage back into Levisham.

18 ROSEDALE ABBEY

THE VALLEY OF ROSEDALE IS ONE OF A STRING OF PARALLEL LENGTHY DALES THAT FLOW SOUTHWARDS FROM THE UPLAND DOME AT THE HEART OF THE NATIONAL PARK, EACH DIVIDED BY MOORLAND RIDGES. THE RIVER SEVEN RUNS A CHARMING COURSE OF SOME 21 MILES TO JOIN THE RIVER RYE IN THE VALE OF PICKERING.

Rosedale Abbey is a lovely village in the true heart of the National Park. It is also a busy little place, with pubs, cafes, shop and caravan sites. Its name stems from the existence of a Cistercian nunnery founded here in the mid-12th century. What little remains stands forlornly in a small enclosure behind the church of St Mary & St Laurence (1839), and is seen at the end of the walk. Much of the remains were plundered for dwellings during the 19th century ironstone boom. Roads radiate from strategically sited Rosedale Abbey, including two which cross the high moors to a range of Eskdale villages.

A remarkable feature of the upper dale was the Rosedale Ironstone Railway, constructed in 1861 to carry iron ore from Rosedale's mines to the furnaces on Teesside. This spectacular achievement of engineering ran across the moors over 1000 feet up, the line having climbed from a different valley by way of a steep incline, then contouring around the head of Farndale to Blakey, overlooking Rosedale itself. Here a junction sent lines around the moor edge to mines on both sides of the dale. The railway closed in 1929 with the demise of mining, but both have left their mark. Today it is difficult to visualise a scene of thousands toiling in this now tranquil dale.

The little community of Rosedale East is a surprising place to find so far up the valley, its existence being due to the ironstone mining era: the terrace of Hill Cottages housed miners, and others survive nearby. The remains of the East Mines featuring some impressive multiple kilns are found just above the hamlet, and the course of the old railway can also be briefly discerned. The Orange Tree relaxation centre was until relatively recently an absorbing Post office/store, one of the last of its breed: the only clue today is a Victorian postbox in its wall. The Methodist Chapel dates from 1872.

THE BASICS

Distance: 4¾ miles / 7.5km

Gradient: One steady climb out of North Dale

Severity: Largely easy walking

Approx. time to walk: 3 hours

Stiles: None

Maps: OS Landranger 94 (Whitby) or Landranger 100 (Malton & Pickering); Explorer OL26 (North York Moors Western area)

Path description: Fieldpaths and quiet lanes

Start Point: Rosedale Abbey village centre (GR SE 724959)

Parking: Central car park (PC YO18 8RT)

Dog friendly: Sheep pastures, dogs preferably on leads

Public toilets: At start

Nearest food: Pubs and cafés at start

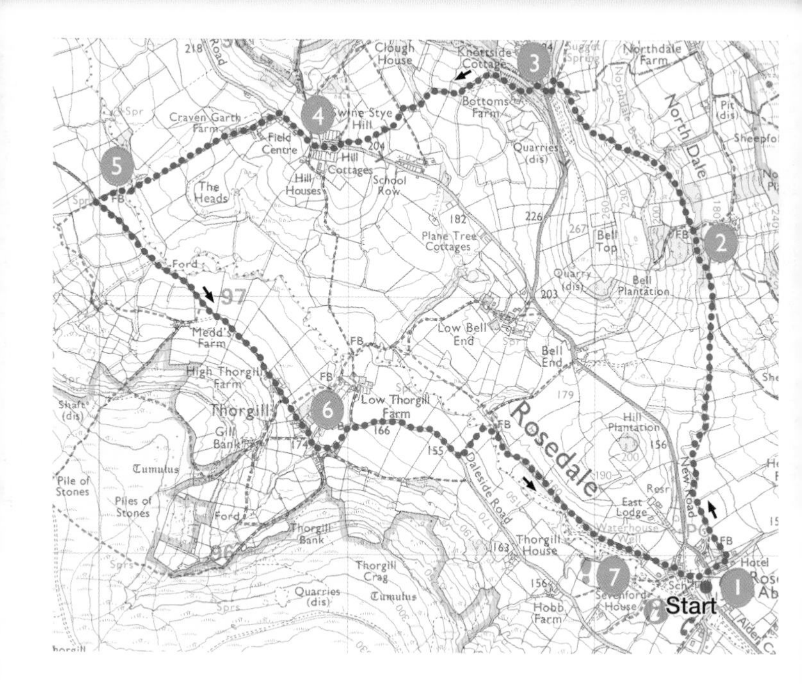

THE ROUTE

1. Leave the crossroads by the green by the Egton road alongside the Milburn Arms. After it enter the car park on the left and leave by a gate ahead. A grass track crosses to a gate, marking the start of a lengthy spell through numerous gates alongside Northdale Beck. After a slab footbridge on a sidestream a guidepost sends a permissive option to a bridle-gate ahead, and a more interesting beckside section soon ensues. Before long you reach a footbridge on the beck.

2. Across, take the path rising with a wall straight ahead, and up on the bank it bears left onto a minor road. Pass straight through an old wall and rise gently away, pathless, to a bridle-gate. Entering rougher terrain, a path now rises alongside a fence to a fence-gate ahead. A hollowed way winds up then along a level course overlooking a pond. Absorbing its access track, this leads up onto a firmer access track just ahead: turn steeply left up this. Quickly easing out, leave by a little path rising to a gate above, onto a road.

3. Turn briefly right and leave by a cart track through a gate on the left into a plantation. Within 50 strides take a thin path dropping left into trees. It quickly swings right, dropping a little and on above Bottoms Farm. Another slant quickly leaves the trees at a bridle-gate onto a green way. Your objective of Hill Cottages

is visible ahead. Through another such gate in front, turn right along the field top to a gate. Now bear left down the field, finding the second gate along in the wall below. Again head along the top, curving left down the far side to a stream. Rise away over a brow, through an old wall corner and cross to a bridle-gate in a fence. A path drops to a footbridge on a reedy stream, rising away up a field edge to a bridle-gate by Hill Cottages, Rosedale East.

4. Joining the road, turn right between the rows to a brow, on past an old chapel to the Orange Tree. Immediately after, turn down an access road past holiday cottages to Craven Garth Farm. Pass through to a gate into the field below and descend two fieldsides. From a corner gate a path slants down to a footbridge on the tree-lined River Seven.

5. Ascend the fieldside to a gate onto an access track, and turn left all the way to Thorgill.

6. Head through the hamlet and follow the traffic-free road out for a few minutes, then take a bridle-gate on the left. A path drops across a field to a bridle-gate accessing another footbridge on the Seven. Across, rise a few paces to a path junction and go right to a bridle-gate out of the trees. The path runs briefly beneath a wooded bank before slanting across the grassy bank, to then run on above trees. Further, it slants gently down to a kissing-gate at the far corner onto a caravan site road alongside Waterhouse Well.

7. Head away along the access road, and immediately past a recreation area, turn briefly left to a kissing-gate onto a road. Emerging opposite the nunnery remains by the church, turn right to the green.

19 LOW MILL

THE VALLEY OF FARNDALE IS ONE OF A STRING OF PARALLEL LENGTHY DALES THAT FLOW SOUTHWARDS FROM THE UPLAND DOME AT THE HEART OF THE NATIONAL PARK, EACH DIVIDED BY SLENDER MOORLAND RIDGES. FARNDALE'S RIVER IS THE DOVE, A BEAUTIFUL STREAM THAT RUNS SOME 19 MILES TO JOIN THE RIVER RYE IN THE VALE OF PICKERING.

Farndale is renowned for its carpet of daffodils, the result being that in early spring you will have little chance to wander lonely as a cloud. Don't be put off by this – it's a lovely stroll and in any case, any crowds will be left behind for the return leg. The reason for this profusion of yellow has been attributed to the monks of Rievaulx and also to Nicholas Postgate, 'martyr of the moors', who dubbed them 'lenten lilies'. Designation of Farndale Nature Reserve in 1953 was almost insufficient to avoid a threatened massive 1960s reservoir a little up-dale: hard to believe that so recently people were still so blind. Opposite the car park is an idyllic picture postcard scene featuring what until 2006 was the Post office, while the corrugated village hall also stands by the car park.

The hamlet of Church Houses is based around the Feversham Arms, while hidden in trees two minutes up the road is St Mary's church. Rebuilt in 1871, a community of friars existed

here in the Middle Ages. Church Houses is also the setting for the annual Farndale Show each August. The return leg from Church Houses through the fields and scattered farms affords superb views across the valley, with the long moorland skyline of Rudland Rigg opposite.

THE BASICS

Distance: 3¼ miles / 5.25km

Gradient: Negligible

Severity: Easy walking

Approx. time to walk: 2½ hours

Stiles: Four

Maps: OS Landranger 94 (Whitby) or Landranger 100 (Malton & Pickering); Explorer OL26 (North York Moors Western area)

Path description: Riverbank and field paths

Start Point: Low Mill village centre (GR SE 672952)

Parking: National Park car park (PC YO62 7JZ)

Dog friendly: Sheep pastures, dogs preferably on leads, make sure they can manage the stiles

Public toilets: At start

Nearest food: Pub and seasonal café at Church Houses, mid-walk

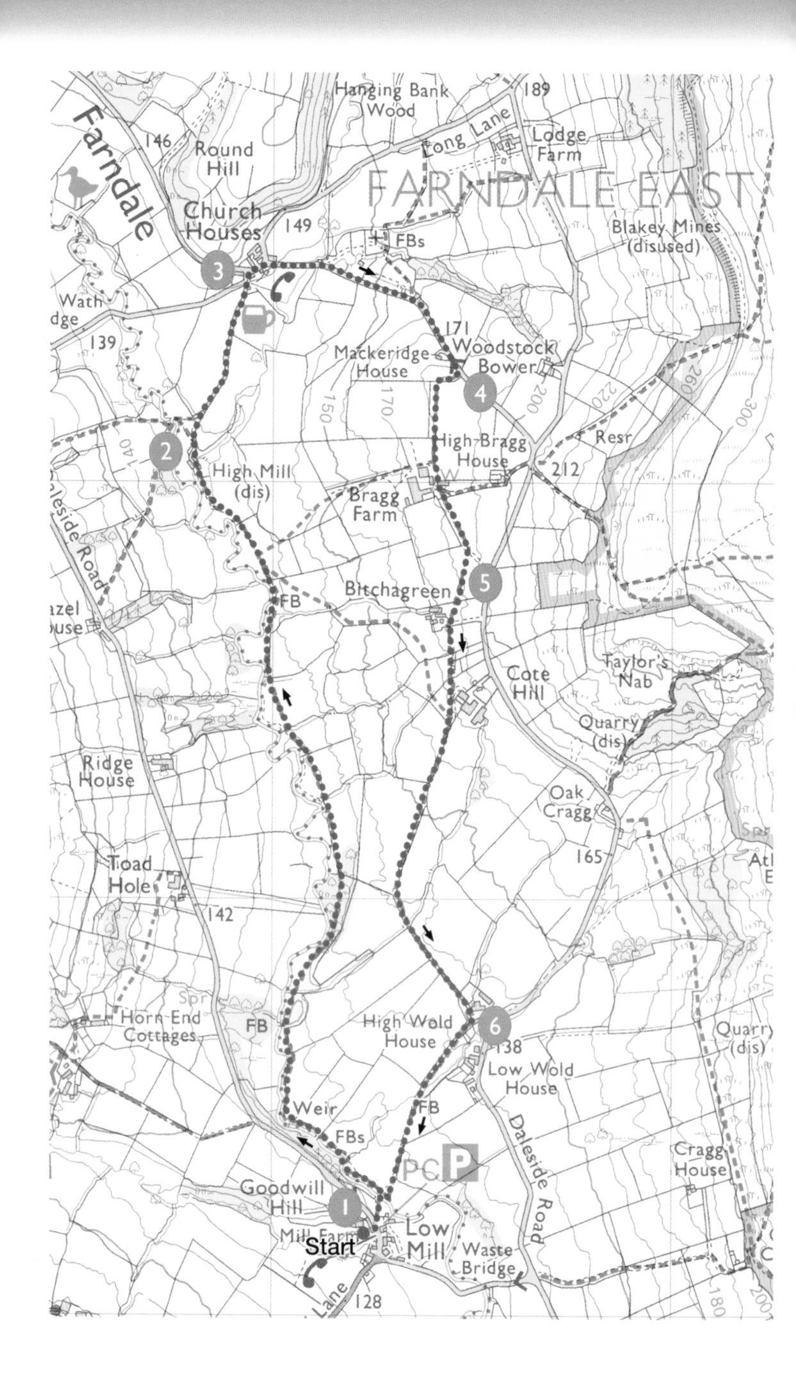
Farndale
Hanging Bank Wood
Long Lane
Lodge Farm
FARNDALE EAST
Round Hill
Church Houses
149
FBs
Blakey Mines (disused)
Wath
139
171
Mackeridge House
Woodstock Bower
High Bragg House
Resr
212
High Mill (dis)
Bragg Farm
Daleside Road
Bitchagreen
FB
Cote Hill
Taylor's Nab
Quarry (dis)
Ridge House
Oak Cragg
165
Toad Hole
142
Horn End Cottages
FB
High Wold House
138
Low Wold House
Quarry (dis)
Weir
FB
FBs
Cragg House
Goodwill Hill
Mill Farm
Start
Low Mill
Waste Bridge
Lane
128
Daleside Road

THE ROUTE

1. From the car park entrance take the adjacent gate to a footbridge over the River Dove. The footpath now follows the Dove upstream, and as this forms the 'daffodil walk' there is little chance of going astray. Note how the meandering Dove covers twice the ground you do! Good views look right up to Blakey Ridge. Various gates are encountered on this path that is solid underfoot all the way to arrival at High Mill. The seasonal Daffy Caffy sits amid this attractive cluster.

2. From High Mill a narrow lane takes you away from the river to Church Houses.

3. Reaching the pub, turn right past a Victorian postbox and keep right at the near immediate fork. The road passes the church set back on the left, then starts a sustained pull, passing the former school on your left.

4. One field beyond the first house on the right, take a gate on the right and head away with the wall on your left to quickly reach a ladder-stile on it. Across, head away with a hedge on your right, and through a gate at the end a track leads along to Bragg Farm. Pass straight through, and keep straight on the access road rising gently away. Before it meets the road however, bear off right at an outer wall corner featuring a redundant stile, and slant across to a ladder-stile over a wall just in front of Bitchagreen.

5. Entering the farmyard, ignore the drive rising left and cross straight over to a gate. Head away along the field tops, crossing a step-stile beneath a house then along to a ladder-stile. Now slant right down beneath the farm at Cote Hill to a gate in the bottom corner. Turn right to descend with the hedge on your left, a grassy track dropping down to a corner gate. Continue down again to a gate, where a track now runs left above a hedge. Through a gate at the end a firmer track forms, running between hedgerows to High Wold House.

6. On entering the farm confines, take a small gate by a larger gate in the right corner ahead. Now descend a narrow pasture with a wall on your right and a tree-lined stream over to your left. At the bottom take the bridle-gate on the left, the briefly enclosed path bridging the stream to emerge via another such gate. Bear gently right away, and as you slant down, a flagged path takes over. This leads down to join a hedge and down to a redundant small gate, beneath which the path swings right to cross to a gate at the footbridge at the start of the walk.

20 HUTTON-LE-HOLE

HUTTON-LE-HOLE IS PROBABLY THE BEST-KNOWN INLAND VILLAGE IN THE NATIONAL PARK, AND IN SUMMER ITS POPULARITY IS ALL TOO EVIDENT. ITS CHARMS ARE OPEN TO VIEW, WITH ITS BECK, BRIDGES AND UBIQUITOUS SHEEP TENDING ITS EXTENSIVE GREENS. THE CROWN INN AND SEVERAL TEAROOMS OFFER REFRESHMENT. THINGS TO LOOK FOR INCLUDE THE OLD CATTLE POUND AND TINY ST CHAD'S CHURCH WITH THE MOUSEMAN'S WORK. HUTTON'S POSITION IS ALSO SUPERB, SHELTERING UNDER THE TABULAR HILLS WITH MOORLAND RISING TO THE NORTH.

Aside from its obvious assets, Hutton's special feature is the Ryedale Folk Museum, whose excellent presentation of local life in bygone days is crowned by a first-class range of reconstructed moor dwellings.

Spaunton is an unassuming street village on a modest ridge: a slender green runs part of its length. Your walk passes the old village pinfold, an 18th century stone enclosure where stray farm animals were held: it was restored in 2012 and is now a Grade II listed building.

Lastingham is a delightful village that shares an identical situation to its neighbour Hutton-le-Hole, sheltering beneath the wooded Tabular Hills while looking north to the moors. Here the similarity ends. Firstly, Lastingham's houses do not stand quietly back, but huddle round a compact centre with lanes branching off in all directions. The second and more notable difference is that in addition to prettiness, Lastingham's pilgrim comes seeking a shrine, that of St Cedd. This Lindisfarne monk founded a monastery in 654, a task completed by his brother Chad. Destroyed by the Danes two centuries later, the site of this important early Christian centre became a place of pilgrimage. In 1078 Stephen of Whitby built a crypt, still intact beneath the present church and a unique Norman relic. Several wells, including one to Cedd, can be found about the village. The Blacksmiths Arms stands in the church's shadow.

THE BASICS

Distance: 4½ miles / 7.25km

Gradient: Only modest uphill sections

Severity: Generally easy walking

Approx. time to walk: 3 hours

Stiles: None

Maps: OS Landranger 94 (Whitby) or Landranger 100 (Malton & Pickering); Explorer OL26 (North York Moors Western area)

Path description: Field and moorland paths, quiet lanes and tracks

Start Point: Hutton-le-Hole village centre (GR SE 704901)

Parking: National Park car park (PC YO62 6UA)

Dog friendly: Sheep pastures and moorland, dogs preferably on leads

Public toilets: At start

Nearest food: Pub and café at start

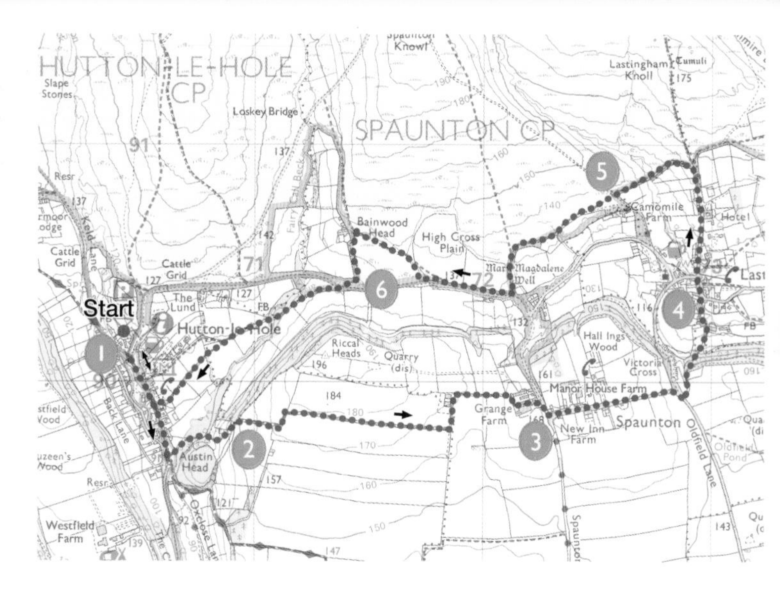

THE ROUTE

1. Leave the village by heading south along the street, passing the pub and museum on your left. On crossing the sidestream of Fairy Call Beck just short of the end, turn sharp left with it to a fence-gate. A path runs briefly upstream through trees, but leave it on a slight knoll by swinging right, passing through one fence-gap and rising to another. Continue briefly up the grassy hollow, then swing left up onto a grassy shelf. Continue straight up a gentler hollow, shortly bearing left to a gate into conifers. Turn briefly right up a grassy path, quickly bearing right to enter a parallel hollow, the old path linking Hutton and Spaunton.

2. Resume along this delightful way, soon bearing right and rising past a ruin out into a field. The grassy track turns sharp left along the edge, quickly turning right to commence a long, hedgeside stride along the crest. Dropping gently to a junction at the end, go left to some barns. Remain on the enclosed cart track which runs right to Grange Farm. Entering its yard, go left down onto a road on the edge of Spaunton.

3. Go right the few strides to a grassy area, then left along the village street. At the end keep straight on to drop to another junction: your way is a footpath signed at the far right side. This curves around to a bridle-gate into woodland, dropping parallel with a sunken way. When the old way swings left, your way drops right, passing through a gate to emerge on the edge of Lastingham. Bear left on the access road out into the centre.

4. Turn briefly left to the corner. With the pub and church just to the left, go straight ahead up the 'no through road' climbing out of the village past Lastingham Grange (refreshments): it ends before a gate onto moorland under Lastingham Knoll. A Millennium stone, guidepost and seat occupy this path crossroads. Turn sharp left to descend a little wallside path through heather to cross a small stream. After a short pull up the other side it runs on to a wall corner above Camomile Farm.

5. Keep straight on the level path across the moor, converging with a fence from the left. Shortly after a wall takes over, the way swings left with it to become enclosed, passing through a gate onto a road. Turn right on its verge, rising slightly then running on to reach grassy moorland on the right. Here turn right on Bainwood farm road. Approaching it, bear left on a small path that drops left near the moor-edge fence, down to two boardwalk sections, over a tiny stream then slanting right though bracken back onto the road.

6. Cross straight over onto an inviting path bearing right with a fence above a bracken bank. At the end is a gate into woodland, and the path drops to a footbridge out of the wood. Emerging into a field, this final stage leads along the edge of a string of fields. The village soon appears ahead, and at the end a small gate puts you into a small area with seats, across which a snicket winds around to emerge onto the village street.

ABOUT THE AUTHOR

Paul Hannon is Yorkshire born and bred, and has been writing about his native county for over 30 years. He has produced around 80 guidebooks to walks in his own and neighbouring counties Lancashire and Cumbria, as well as cycling and general guides, and has contributed to numerous magazines.

A keen photographer, he is currently making greater use of his extensive photographic archive to develop an exhaustive picture library dedicated to all things Yorkshire. 'Journey of the Wharfe' is part of an ongoing series of hardback colour titles celebrating the life and landscape of the great rivers of Yorkshire.

A father of three grown-up children, he still lives within a stone's throw of his hometown of Keighley. When not walking and photographing, his interests include Bradford City FC, ornithology and good beer.

As a serious hillwalker he has climbed hundreds of mountains in the British Isles. In 1991 he completed the 214 Lake District 'Wainwright' fells, and in 2007 became a proud Munroist on completing the 284 Scottish 3000ft peaks on his 50th birthday.